PRAYERWALKING

'Walking the land in prayer is preparing the way for unprecedented growth of the church in this country.'
LYNN GREEN, Regional Director, Youth With A Mission, Middle East and Africa, and joint organiser of March for Jesus

'Perspiring and practical prayer! A must for anyone interested in revival.'
SANDY MILLAR, Vicar of Holy Trinity Church, Brompton Road, London

'Visionary, inspiring, powerful – simple and practical, so easy to fit into our everyday lifestyle.'
CHRIS LEAGE, UK Co-ordinator, Lydia Fellowship

'Jesus said to watch and pray – this book takes that command literally. I highly recommend it. We have practised these principles for some time now, and it has changed our lives.'
FLOYD McCLUNG, Executive Director, International Operations, Youth With A Mission

'Prayer involves talking, but increasingly we are going to see prayer involve walking. To reach the nation with the gospel by the year 2000 we must soak our land in prayer. *Prayerwalking* will help us do just that.'
GERALD COATES, Leader of Pioneer Team and joint organiser of March for Jesus

'*Prayerwalking* – as old as the Bible, vital for spiritual warfare, a catalyst for an advancing church.'
ROGER FORSTER, Leader of Ichthus Fellowship, London

'Discover in this simple, practical manual a key that I believe God is giving to us as a nation.'
IAN TRAYNAR, Worship leader, songwriter and Director of CMA Personal Membership Ltd

D1439225

To all those who walked, ran, limped,
and above all prayed
from John O'Groats to Land's End
during Summer 1989.

Prayerwalking

Graham Kendrick
and
John Houghton

MAKE WAY MUSIC

KINGSWAY PUBLICATIONS

EASTBOURNE

Biblical quotations are from the
Revised Authorised Version copyright © Thomas Nelson Inc. 1982

The text of the Apostles' Creed is copyright
© International Consultation on English Texts 1970, 1971, 1975

Cover and text design by Ron Bryant Funnell
Cartoons by Mike Kazybrid
Cover photograph by Jack Nielsen
Text photos by John Houghton

British Library Cataloguing in Publication Data

Kendrick, Graham
Prayerwalking.
1. Christian life. Prayer
I. Title II. Houghton, John, 1944–
248.32

ISBN 0-86065-870-8

Make Way Music, Glyndley Manor, Stone Cross
Pevensey, East Sussex BN24 5BS

Printed in Great Britain for
KINGSWAY PUBLICATIONS LTD
1 St Anne's Road, Eastbourne, E Sussex BN21 3UN by
Stanley L Hunt (Printers) Ltd, Rushden, Northants

CONTENTS

This manual is designed to challenge and teach, and to be used practically.

Interspersed in the main text you will find useful teaching modules and tips, designed to enhance your desire to pray and to clear up some of the common difficulties which Christians encounter in prayer. Towards the end are a number of prayerwalk plans which are intended for your actual use 'on the road', together with some pages on which you can jot down prayer requests and the date they were answered.

For this reason we recommend that every member of your prayerwalk group has their own copy of this manual.

Introducing

a Dynamic Strategy for
PRAYER!

Handle this book with care! It could prove to be dynamite in your hands. For in these pages we are aiming at nothing less than a spiritual revolution across the industrialised world; a revolution of life patterns which will transform and remobilise the prayer life of the Christian church.

There is no issue more vital. Christian leaders throughout the world recognise with increasing urgency that lack of effective intercession is the major weakness of the church in the industrialised nations. Recent decades have seen many changes in the way churches operate. New forms of worship have developed, home groups are now commonplace, evangelistic activities have multiplied and leadership structures have been re-evaluated. All this has brought its measure of blessing. But it has not brought revival, nor turned the bleak tide of secularism. An often compromised church has made only small gains for all its internal reshufflings.

Ask church leaders the reason and they will point at once to the prayer meeting. It is almost inevitably the poorest attended meeting of the week. Question most believers on the aspect of their Christian lives they feel most ashamed about and they will confess to having difficulty with effective prayer. Lack of opportunity, lack of motivation, lack of direction – in spite of the fact that we have created more potential free time than any previous generation in history.

Everyone knows we ought to pray more; most of us find it difficult. Our dependence on the clock and on saving time to do more things flies right in the face of stillness, meditation and waiting on the Lord. The pressure is on us to be out and about, to meet the deadline, to catch the train, to get the kids to school, to listen to the news.... We work hard and long. Exhausted we sit down to pray. Not surprisingly, our thoughts wander, we drift off to sleep. Or we simply feel too restless to concentrate and we get up to do something else.

Prayer meetings themselves are no help. Often boring and predictable, we find them unattractive. We don't know how to take part. Prayers seem so long and so repetitious. It's easier to watch the TV, and hope the guilt goes away.

We need a revolution! Something must challenge our existing life patterns if we are ever to resolve our prayerlessness. That's where this book comes in. We want to introduce you to a concept which will set your prayer life ablaze and release you into effective, sustained, challenging intercession. Almost everyone can do it, and that includes all of us who feel our prayer lives are something of a failure. So, prepare yourself to be transformed by the radical (if not completely new) notion of PRAYERWALKING!

We need a revolution!

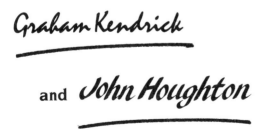

Graham Kendrick

and *John Houghton*

1

The Balance of Our Prayers

Praying is like breathing – in either case, people who don't are dead! No prayer, no life. It's as simple as that, both for the individual and for the church.

It also holds true for our nation. The life and well-being of society depends on our prayers. The third-century Christian defender of the faith, Tertullian, recognised this when he wrote, 'Without ceasing, we offer prayer for all our emperors. We pray for them long life; for security to the empire; for protection to the imperial house; for brave armies, a faithful senate, an honest people, a world at peace – everything, which as man or Caesar, an emperor would wish' (A*pology*).

Praying is like breathing

The importance of our prayers was brought home to us with a fresh sense of urgency through a recent shared vision which occurred during a time of worship while we were prayerwalking en route for London and the 'March for Jesus across the Nation' event in September 1989.

Graham had begun to sing a prophetic song lamenting the wasted lives and bleak futures of people without Christ. The refrain majored on the line: 'Hanging in the balance of our prayers'.

At the same time, John was receiving a vision of a great portent in the skies. It was of a giant pair of scales, heavily weighed down on one side by a pan overflowing with blood, guts, excrement, vomit and filth. The other pan hung high and dry. Another of the team was quite independently seeing an enormous pair of scales as well.

Then a teardrop fell from heaven and it wet the empty pan. Another fell, and another, until the pan began to fill with tears. As it did so, the filth began to slide off the other pan, and slowly the scales tipped.

Then, from the pan of tears there sprang a river which flooded right across the nation and washed away all the filth and vileness, until the land was cleansed.

The scene changed to reveal thousands of little white coffins and white crosses. Families stood before them, united. Wan smiles broke through the sadness of their faces. They had at last buried their dead. The 'war' was over;

Help for the helpless

Ever since the serpent tempted Eve with, 'You will be like God,' humans have sought to live independent of God. This idolatrous pride in ourselves is the greatest single barrier to fellowship with him. Humble trust in Christ clears the way. O. Hallesby wrote, 'Only he who is helpless can truly pray.'

peace had come to their land. In spite of the casualties, there was hope and joy for the future.

We felt the Lord was saying that revival and healing will come to the nation as God's people pray. Like Jesus, we must identify not only with triumph but also with the suffering of the lost. The tears of prayer are ours, but they are also the tears of heaven. The message is plain: the fate of the nation hangs in the balance of our prayers.

▢

Christians everywhere acknowledge that the church is urgently in need of a revitalised prayer life. One of the most significant responses to this need is that many are becoming stirred to walk and pray. As a result, they are experiencing a remarkable release of effective intercession in their lives and churches . . . .

— 2 —
Prayerwalking Is a Strategy

... for breaking the mould

Think of a traditional church prayer meeting. Nine times out of ten it brings to mind images of a dull, routine gathering, often lacking in real vision and direction. Such a meeting may have been going for years and it is almost certainly attended by somewhat less than the majority of church members. Those who do attend faithfully often just cannot get out of the rut; the rest seldom find the motivation to get in. It's no way to change a nation, that's for sure.

Prayerwalking, by its very nature, breaks the mould of the static meeting. It automatically provides a constant challenge and fresh stimulus to effective corporate intercession, and just about every Christian can take part, including all those who have never really made it to the traditional prayer meeting.

... for taking the walls off the church

Prayerwalking aims to achieve in the realm of prayer what Make Way Marches have sought to do in the realm of praise and worship. That is, to get the church outside its buildings in spiritual and numerical strength.

The world today could easily be excused for thinking that the church is some strange mystery religion. Just what do we get up to behind the walls of those intimidating buildings? How many unbelievers in your locality have actually ever seen a real Christian pray?

Prayerwalking takes the church to the outside world. Although the primary aim is not focused on evangelism, inevitably people ask you what you are doing and usually take considerable interest when you tell them you are praying for their locality. It's not that unusual for a passer-by to ask you to pray for them.

. . . for taking the walls off the church

... for unpremeditated evangelism

Closely related to the above is the fact that you do meet real, ordinary people when you are out prayerwalking. We keep hearing stories of meaningful conversations developing, some of which are leading to conversion.

On one particular occasion we found ourselves in conversation with some Czech backpackers. They had some musical instruments, so we finished up having an impromptu sing-song. It allowed us to share Jesus with them and give them a Bible, only months before political liberalisation began to release their nation to the gospel.

Many Christians today long to see signs and wonders performed in the name of Jesus on our streets. A prayerwalk provides an ideal opportunity. You may well feel led to witness to a passer-by whom the Lord has just laid on your heart. He may be saved, or healed, or both! Prayerwalking provides that crucial ingredient: being there.

... for increasing our awareness

Many Christians pray for their neighbourhood but never actually encounter it. We don't know what's there because we don't do the leg-work to find out. In Hailsham, as a result of a prayerwalk one evening, we discovered that many young people hang around the shopping precinct because they've nothing else to do, so we opened an evangelistic coffee bar for them. Since doing so we have seen miraculous healings and numbers of socially deprived teenagers saved.

. . . for increasing our awareness

Through prayerwalking, Christians are discovering roads they never knew existed, local clubs and institutions of which they had been unaware and people in all the diversity of their human condition and need. Prayerwalking 'earths' our heavenly intercessions.

Prayerwalk News . . .

They wanted a fight. Revenge. Anything. One of them, already with a broken nose, had just been slashed across the face with a knife. Things looked nasty. The gang seethed with growing anger in the town square.

What should the Christians do? They ran the evangelistic coffee bar outside which the incident had occurred. A nurse reckoned he needed five stitches, but he was a big guy and refused to go to hospital. Hailsham Christian Fellowship had founded the coffee bar as the result of a prayerwalk. That was to be the answer now.

Speaking out loud in tongues, two of their number began to circle the mob. They asked the Lord to take control of the situation. Out of the blue, the ruling peace of God descended on the gang. Now docile, the whole

... for enlarging our vision

It's very easy for our vision to be limited by our present activities. Prayerwalking will open up whole new vistas. For example, we will find ourselves praying for other churches, for local governments, for schools, prisons, hospitals, as well as specific homes and shops – all of which we may well have overlooked in the past.

. . for enlarging our vision

Environment affects all of us. Get out of doors to pray and we only have to look upwards to become aware of the greatness of our God. 'The heavens declare the glory of God; and the firmament shows his handiwork' (Ps 19:1). A new sense of the majesty of the Lord and of his eternal purposes will inspire us to pray, not only for our own nation, but for the whole world.

... for invading Satan's territory

The notion of a territorial spiritual government raises all sorts of theological questions. Without wishing to answer those questions in this manual, we none the less reject the philosophy which denies the spiritual significance of our mortal bodies and the material world. It is not Christian thinking to see things only in 'spiritual' terms. In Scripture, the spiritual and the material are intimately entwined. Jesus is 'the Word made flesh'.

Hence, centres of earthly power are inevitably centres of satanic interest. The New Testament recognised that to be the case with both Jerusalem and Rome. John wrote to the church at Pergamos, '...where you dwell, where Satan's throne is' (Rev 2:13).

Prayerwalking takes us bodily and spiritually into territory where Satan has a vested interest. We are invited to wreak havoc among those interests in the name of Jesus.

---

crowd returned quietly to the coffee bar.

It was not over yet. The two believers offered to pray for the man right there on the street. They knelt down and asked God to heal his nose. A miracle occurred. 'It doesn't hurt anymore,' he cried, tapping his nose. 'Wow, this stuff's good!' Off came the plaster. The deep gash had vanished except for a small mark. Not even a drop of blood remained.

Since then the man has begun his journey towards Christ.

★★★

If you have significant prayerwalking testimonies to tell, we would like to hear from you. Send your story, preferably typed, to John Houghton, c/o the publishers.

Beat the devil!

You don't have to be a Christian for very long before you discover there's a war going on and you are part of it. Paul told us to take the armour of God so as to fight victoriously (Eph 6:10-18).

The passage ends with these words: 'Praying always with all prayer and supplication in the Spirit, being watchful to this end with all perseverance and supplication for all the saints.'

> Satan trembles when he sees
> The weakest saint upon his knees

Whether in our personal lives or in society, spiritual victory over the devil and his hosts depends upon our prayers. Not surprisingly, he doesn't like it when we pray, so he'll do all he can to sabotage our prayer lives.

Sabotage technique one: distraction

It's not hard to be distracted from prayer in our generation. What with the television and the phone, people calling and staying late, the Saturday night party, too much work, the kids and so on, it's easy to lose the time we wanted to give to God.

Then, when we do attempt to pray, we find our thoughts wandering all over the place and wonder why we bothered in the first place. It's a very simple strategy for preventing us praying.

Jesus, in the Garden of Gethsemane, said to his disciples, 'Watch and pray, lest you enter into temptation. The spirit indeed is willing, but the flesh is weak' (Mt 26:41). Keep alert! The Enemy is subtle. He'll weary you with distractions. Take authority over your situation in the name of Jesus. Battle through! Be firm with the off switch, don't stay out so late, get up earlier, even change your job perhaps. It's essential that you pray.

Wandering thoughts can be dealt with in several ways. The simplest is to pray about them as they come to mind. After all, these are the things that clearly concern you, otherwise you wouldn't be thinking about them in the first place.

Praying out loud and praying Scripture back to God helps enormously. You might also revise your lifestyle so that you build 'thinking time' into it, quite apart from 'praying time'.

Sabotage technique two: discouragement

Jesus said we should always pray and not give up. He knew that it would be hard work and himself wrestled in prayer before God. The spiritual saboteur will take full advantage of that fact and do his best to discourage us in the battle.

As with any battle there are good times and bad times. Understandably, we grow discouraged when our prayers appear not to be answered. The circumstances of our life may be sad and difficult. We may be under persecution and feel all alone. But all this must be distinguished from that unnatural depression which makes us feel the Christian life isn't worth it, or which makes us despair of ourselves and our praying. That's from the Evil One.

Recognise the source. Satan is opposing you. Fight back in the Lord's strength. James said, 'Submit to God. Resist the devil and he will flee from you. Draw near to God and he will draw near to you' (Jas 4:7-8). We can overcome our Enemy with the Lord's help. Fight on, Christian soldier, and do not be discouraged!

... for redeeming the time

Many Christians, with all the benefits of cars and automatic washing machines
– which theoretically should create leisure space – still complain that they
haven't time to pray. The reason is a simple one. We are surrounded by
'time thieves'.

Number one is, of course, the TV. There are others: the telephone,
newspapers and magazines, the car, the home computer. These things steal
frightening amounts of our time with all the subtlety of a pickpocket. You
don't know the time has gone until you need it for something important, like
prayer.

The Bible commands us to pray without ceasing (1 Thess 5:17).
Prayerwalking releases us from those 'time thieves' so that we can better fulfil
this command. Perhaps not surprisingly, it also improves our lifestyle so that
we actually find we have more time at our disposal than before.

God doesn't shout

God doesn't shout and run after us in order to get our attention, as though
he were an insecure schoolboy desperately trying to hang on to our friend-
ship. He says we have to seek his face. 'Be still, and know that I am God'
(Ps 46:10). 'Draw near to God and he will draw near to you' (Jas 4:8). If God
ever seems distant it is because we have moved, not he.

Do you want to grow in the knowledge of God? Then give yourself to
prayer.

If we want to know what our marriage partners or best friends think, we
ask them. Years of practice mean that we usually know what they want!
Similarly, the knowledge and will of God is only a mystery if we don't
discuss it with him. Occasional flashes of insight are no substitute for a
sustained prayer relationship in which you get to know what he is thinking.

... for inhabiting our streets with righteousness

The psalmist longed for a day when there would be no cry of distress in our
streets (Ps 144:14). It was said of the Whitefield/Wesleyan revival that such was
the benign influence of the gospel that an unaccompanied woman and child
could journey the length of Great Britain without fear of molestation. That
guarantee could not be given in our own day.

Violence occurs in our streets because they are virtually empty of all
except the solitary victim and the lurking assailant. Gangs govern street
corners because there is no competition. The righteous are either shut up in
their houses or hurtling past in their cars.

Getting righteous people out on the streets praying, as a regular part of life, is one of the most effective ways we have of freeing our towns and cities from the scourge of robbery, rape and violence. By such prayer we can change the spiritual 'balance of power' and make our streets safe places for people to walk. It's a great way to restore a sense of community.

When you are unsure of
what to pray about, try
praying Bible verses back
to God.

... for improving our fellowship

There is no sweeter fellowship than that found in
worshipping and praying together. Although
prayerwalking is certainly to be encouraged solo,
some of its best effects are experienced when
undertaken corporately.

A small group regularly prayerwalking will
draw very close to one another in spirit.
Misunderstandings are more easily resolved in the
relaxed environment which exists for
prayerwalkers. Even those who hardly know one
another will find relationships forming with
remarkable ease over a very short period of time.

Prayerwalking is constructive work performed
together. The labourers can enjoy the team
satisfaction of a job done well and look forward to
the shared fruit of their labours.

Holy motives

Those who don't pray will never know the truth about themselves. Consequently they can never really change for the better. Prayer involves us in a process of purifying our motives. The apostle James wrote, 'You ask and do not receive, because you ask amiss, that you may spend it on your pleasures' (Jas 4:3). When prayers are unanswered we start asking leading questions about our motives!

... for 'total-being' spiritual activity

We hear a lot about wholeness and holistic techniques nowadays. When these ideas come from the erroneous New Age Movement they should be thoroughly avoided. But the Bible speaks often of a wholeness, well-being or *shalom* (translated 'peace') which comes through the gospel. No part of our being is excluded from the blessing of God. He wants to sanctify us completely – spirit, soul and body (1 Thess 5:23).

Prayerwalking, involving as it does every aspect of our being, is a wonderful way of fulfilling God's holy will for our lives. We have had wonderful experiences on the road when not only our minds and spirits are engaged in intercession, but even the physical energies of our bodies are expressing the prayer burden – true body-language, no less!

. . . for 'total being'
spiritual activity

Prayer problem-solver   **1**

How do you address God?

How should we speak to God? Older Christians sometimes still use Shakespearian English, feeling that it carries a due reverence for God and reflects the nobility of the King James Version of the Bible with which they are familiar. Others have reacted to this and adopt a 'my pal God' approach in order to stress the reality and intimacy of their relationship with God.

Integrity is what really counts. Jesus warned us against using vain repetition (Mt 6:7). True prayer springs from an honest heart, and the words we use should reflect both what we feel and what God is like. Read the Psalms and other great prayers in the Bible and learn from them how to speak to God.

Should we speak out loud or 'in our minds'? It doesn't much matter. Prayer was usually spoken audibly in the Bible and it has the great merit of greatly reducing the problem of wandering thoughts.

There is a deeper side to this, too. Not only are we to taste the excitement and thrill of this kind of praying, we are also to enter the pain and suffering of a lost humanity in the sacrifice of prayer. Prayerwalking in adverse conditions will help us identify, albeit in a small way, with the passion of Christ of whom it is written, 'being in agony, he prayed more earnestly. And his sweat became like great drops of blood falling down to the ground' (Lk 22:44). Needless to say, the pain dimension is more likely to be our experience on the twentieth mile of the day on a prayer pilgrimage than on a suburban two-miler.

Give me patience!

God delights to answer prayers like, 'Lord, give me patience!' The answer will not come from a book, however, but from life. Testings, prayers which are not answered instantly, will all work perseverance into our souls.

Jesus told the parable of the persistent widow (Lk 18:1-8) for the express purpose of teaching us that we 'always ought to pray and not lose heart'. Persistent prayer develops the strength and stamina of our souls.

— 3 —
Why Walk?

At the dawn of time the Lord God walked the estates of Eden in sweet fellowship with Adam and Eve. Jared's son, Enoch, walked with God and somehow never stopped until he had walked right out of this world and into heaven. Noah walked with God and built an ark. Abraham was commanded to walk the length and breadth of the Promised Land. Together with Isaac he walked up Mount Moriah and discovered the Lord's provision for salvation. Moses walked the desert and met God at the burning bush. This was good preparation for leading a stubborn people on a forty-year walk to the Promised Land, and when they got there, who can forget Joshua's walk around Jericho? Isaiah the prophet spent three years walking naked and barefoot as a sign against the untrustworthy kingdoms of Egypt and Ethiopia.

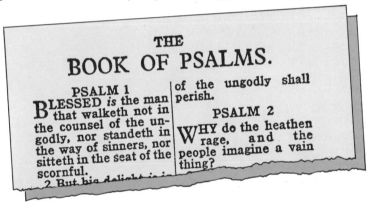

THE
BOOK OF PSALMS.

PSALM 1
BLESSED *is* the man that walketh not in the counsel of the ungodly, nor standeth in the way of sinners, nor sitteth in the seat of the scornful.
2. But his delight is

of the ungodly shall perish.

PSALM 2
WHY do the heathen rage, and the people imagine a vain thing?

So basic is walking to human existence that the Scriptures use it as the most common metaphor to describe human conduct. Psalm 1 opens, typically, 'Blessed is the man who walks not in the counsel of the ungodly,' while, in the New Testament, Paul exhorts us to 'walk in the Spirit' (Gal 5:16).

To walk is the aspiration of every baby, and to teach a child to walk is the proud privilege of every parent. God appeals to his wayward people on the basis of his loving parenthood. 'I taught Ephraim to walk...' (Hos 11:3).

When Jesus came into the world he did so as a walker. He might have ridden a GTX donkey or driven a turbo-powered chariot, but preferred instead to use his legs. With just three years to minister, speed was apparently not of the essence to Jesus – rather different from many of today's jet-setting ministries.

Today, we have to persuade people of the benefits of walking. In the industrialised world, leg-power has been largely replaced by motor car-power. The ease, comfort and speed of our four-wheeled chariots makes them seem indispensable for even a short trip round the corner. But there is a price to pay.

Quite apart from the tax, insurance, petrol, repairs and depreciation, there is the price of health, inner peace and well-being – and a cost to our sense of community.

TAKING THE CAR INSTEAD OF WALKING

THE BILL

Weaker muscles, especially feet, legs, abdomen, lower back, heart and lungs.

Increased proneness to sedentary complaints, especially obesity, poor circulation, varicose veins, heart disease, chest complaints, head colds and sinusitis, poor digestion, lowered sexual vitality.

Build-up of tension, thereby contributing to a whole range of diseases from cancer and heart attacks to ulcers and arthritis.

Stressed relationships arising from failure to dissipate tension.

Loss of wisdom through lack of creative thinking time.

Sense of constant busy-ness and loss of inner rest.

Detachment from creation and its glories in favour of artificiality.

Isolation from society leading to excessive individualism, loneliness and unreality.

TOTAL | VERY EXPENSIVE

Accountant's recommendation: It is unquestionably healthier to walk!

Walking restores the natural rhythm to life. It allows the mind and spirit freedom to work in harmony with the body. The slower pace of walking results in a deliberate creation of space in our busy lives – a bit like those mysterious *selahs* in the psalms where perhaps we are meant to meditate creatively.

The harmony induced by walking eases tensions and allows our inner being to recover from the stress of Westernised life. We have time to think out our problems and to plan for the future. We create the potential for a more fruitful relationship with God.

Against the clock

This is not an age suited to prayer and meditation, particularly in the industrialised nations. There are two primary reasons for this, and it's as well to understand them if we are to revitalise our prayer lives.

The first is the possessive materialism of our times. We have created a world in which the seen is of more value than the unseen. Spiritual awareness is hard to come by in a world of advertising and avarice, of microchips and machines. Technical progress appears able to solve all our problems. It also drains our inner resources as we seek to acquire, to maintain and protect, let alone use all these things. Christians don't despise the material world; indeed, we recognise God's providence in supplying material blessings. But we set limits, 'For what advantage is it to a man if he gains the whole world, and is himself destroyed or lost?' (Lk 9:25).

We must make a conscious effort to open ourselves up to the spiritual dimensions of life, and yet do so in the midst of the culture around us. As we shall see, prayerwalking provides a wonderful opportunity to re-educate our values and our perceptions.

The other cultural hindrance we face is to do with our view of time. Ever since the Industrial Revolution we have been committed to accurate synchronised timekeeping and constant productive output—because machines run best like that, the manpower that serves the machine must do likewise.

The effect has been to breed a society in which people do not sit around meditating. That's wasteful, inefficient, unproductive. Everything must move with purpose. We must be doing something.

Our clever machines have created leisure. A wonderful idea. The trouble is, we can't use our leisure for prayer and meditation. Our social conditioning says we've got to be doing something more useful, more interesting. Prayer is 'wasting time'.

The result is a society which is tired but restless, and which has denied its appetite for God. Frenetic activists following every kind of trivial pursuit, we can't stop. We can't even live without background sound any more.

Is there an answer? Yes, we believe there is. Prayerwalking provides a constructive channelling for the restlessness of our driven society. It will also re-educate us into a more healthy lifestyle. We will discover how to transform that most precious possession which we call time and use it with real effectiveness in the purposes of God.

When your thoughts wander, write them down and pray about them.

The mild rhythmic exercise which walking provides (unless you are a fanatic) is an excellent and almost painless way of toning up the body. It is one of the best antidotes to the ailments produced by our increasingly sedentary society.

Walking introduces us to another world. It is a world of mortality and vulnerability, of simplicity and humanity; one which we largely rush by in our constant haste to be somewhere else. Walking gives us a fresh awareness of our environment and of people. Yes, there are people out there. In fact, an enormous number, most of whom do not frequent our motor-driven churches. Perhaps there's a connection between these facts?

Above all, walking can revolutionise our personal devotions and the prayer life of our church by combining it with prayer.

Pray more, grow more

God wants all his children to reach spiritual maturity. Prayer and testings are the means he uses. Sinless though he was, even Jesus went through this process. 'In the days of his flesh, when he had offered up prayers and supplications, with vehement cries and tears to him who was able to save him from death, and was heard because of his godly fear, though he was a Son, yet he learned obedience by the things which he suffered' (Heb 5:7-9).

Only those brought to their knees on earth are qualified to sit on the throne in heaven.

— 4 —
Can Prayer and Walking Really Be Combined?

In a word, yes. You don't have to be stationary or in a room in order to pray. Jesus' words given in the Sermon on the Mount about avoiding street corners and going into the privacy of our rooms for prayer (Mt 6:5-7) were addressed not against prayerwalking but against hypocrisy and men-pleasing. He himself took many journeys, often alone, into deserted places in order to pray (eg Lk 5:16). It would be foolish to imagine that he didn't start praying until he reached his lonely destination in the middle of nowhere.

Can prayer and walking really be combined?

The idea of prayerwalking is nothing new. In times past when walking was the general mode of transport it was perfectly normal for Christians to pray as they travelled. As far back as AD 180, Hermas writes in *The Shepherd*, 'While then I am walking alone, I entreat the Lord that he will accomplish the revelations and the visions which he showed me through his holy Church, that he may strengthen me and may give repentance to his servants which have stumbled, that his great and glorious name may be glorified.'

Succat (b. AD 385), later known as St Patrick, while a swineherd, said, 'The Spirit urged me to such a degree that I poured forth as many as a hundred prayers in one day. And even during the night, in the forests and on the mountains where I kept my herd, the rain, and snow, and frost, and sufferings which I endured, excited me to seek after God.'

Arguably, John Wycliffe's fourteenth-century itinerant preachers, the Lollards, received such a title (the word comes from the Dutch *lollen*, to mumble [prayers]) because they were always praying as they walked. The Lollard movement lasted three centuries and resulted in that great spiritual revival which we call the Reformation.

George Fox entered Lichfield walking barefoot, praying and burning with the prophetic word, 'Woe to the bloody city of Lichfield!' to learn later that he was raising up a spiritual memorial to a thousand martyrs slain over a thousand years earlier.

Prayer changes things

It is often said that prayer changes things. Certainly it does. We suspect that it changes *us*, but does it change the mind of God?

Some believers have made heavy weather of this in their desire to uphold the sovereignty of God. In the process they have become fatalists in prayer, reducing it almost to an academic exercise—God is going to do it anyway.

That isn't the picture the Bible gives us. There we see a dynamic inter-action between the Lord and his people. Prayer is never just going through the motions to satisfy the immutable will of God. Rather, he has chosen to accommodate us and our praying in his eternal will in such a way that prayer really can change things. We have a God who chooses to be persuadable—and that is the marvel of divine grace! Sound Christian theology recognises that he works in partnership with our prayers, neither as a puppet on the end of our string, nor as a remorseless pre-programmed machine, but as a loving heavenly Father responding to his children.

This being so, blessing is released through our prayers... and if we don't pray, then blessing is withheld.

Christians today are again learning to set aside time for protracted periods of intercession. Some travel to mountains, others gather in forests and market squares, yet others in homes and halls. Many are beginning to walk and pray. We are recovering no less than a major heritage of the church.

Right now the Lord is honouring the spirit of intercession with an outpouring of blessing upon many lands. Tens of thousands are coming to Christ. We in our frenetic, materialistic, techno-society desperately need an effective prayer strategy if we are to share in those blessings. Prayerwalking provides just that.

Prayer problem-solver

2

What's the best position for praying?

You can pray to God in any position you like—even hanging upside down from a rope half-way down a mineshaft if you wish. You'd probably want to pray then, in any case! In Scripture, people adopted a posture suitable to how they felt. Standing was the most common, but kneeling and prostration were also used—and of course walking. The most unusual was sitting because that posture was reserved for when the job was done. Hence, Jesus 'sat down' at the right hand of God when he had accomplished our salvation.

You can pray with your eyes open or closed—preferably open if you are out walking. The only merit in 'hands together and eyes closed' is to avoid distractions and fidgeting—perhaps suited to children, but hardly to adults!

— 5 —
We Walked the Land

A soft grey morning greets the small party of walkers as they gather at **The Mound, Edinburgh.** The date: 29th August 1989. Fringe Festival time, but this group is so 'fringe' that neither their arrival nor their departure is noted by more than a few well-wishers.

A simple torch-lighting ceremony, raising no more than an indifferent eyebrow from passers-by, and we are off. Our aim is a simple one: to walk from

Edinburgh to London, 480 miles by the route we are given, and to pray for every mile of the way. Already Christians have run, walked and prayed from John O'Groats down to Edinburgh. We pick up the flame from them.

A week or so later another party sets off from Land's End, Cornwall, with the same intent. We will meet together in London on 16th September, the day of the March for Jesus rallies.

It's an odd feeling, doing something special, different, while life bustles on in its normal fashion all around. Here we are, striding through busy towns and cities, pacing long dusty roads, while cars and lorries hurtle about their business with no more than a curious glance at our fluorescent jackets and determined faces, and yet we feel we are involved in one of the most significant projects any of us has ever undertaken.

Groups of people join us on the way, all motivated and inspired by the burden to pray for the nation. They are marvellous, feeding us with local information, encouraging us in our endeavour and even on occasion washing our weary feet! They feel something significant is happening.

One Christian lady out shopping in East Birmingham who knows nothing of our coming, suddenly feels God say to her that something of spiritual importance is happening nearby. She jumps in the car and drives around until she finds our team. A few more minutes and we would be gone, but our prayers have made an impact.

As we journey, similar words are given to us by people whose only connection is with the Lord.

'I see a spinal column, but the nerves are damaged, so the messages from the head fail to reach the body. Such is the state of the church. As you walk and pray, the nerves are being restored, and the synapses, those interfaces between leaders, are being healed.'

'You are walking down a dry river-bed, but behind you is rushing a wall of white water. Ahead of you is a cabin built over a spring. Its builders should have built a boat to ride the stream, for the cabin will be swept away in the tide of blessing which is to come.'

'You are like a lawn-mower cutting a swathe through difficult terrain. You will make it easier for others to walk the path of prayer in the future.'

We enter a world hitherto hidden from our busy Christian lives. It is the world of powerful praying while on the move – total body praying. We begin to experience a new freedom in prayer, a fresh awareness of the Lord's presence, a greater reality and prophetic clarity in our intercessions. Somehow the combination of moderate physical exercise, ever-changing scenery, companionship in Christ and the process of continuous praying releases something in our spirits. The Spirit of God is manifestly upon our praying.

This world is one that touches earth and links it to heaven. Moving at a slower pace we find we have more time to hear and to observe. We feel in touch with reality. Even an awareness of the weather teaches us that life is not controlled by fast cars, satellite links and computers. These things are only the toys with which children play, while God's great plans roll by unhindered.

We find people on the streets – lots of them. Ordinary folk, often the marginalised of our society, who are suddenly accessible to our prayers and our conversations. How else would Jesus meet them today, other than the way he did 2,000 years ago?

We begin to appreciate something else. What we and our companions are doing is prophetic. It's not an end in itself, but a beginning. God wants to release his people throughout the nation into walking and praying. Our dreams grow; could this happen right across Europe and the United States of America? Millions of God's people regularly walking and praying in their localities could change the face of the Westernised world. If prayer is the key to revival, this could surely open the lock!

Believe you me!

Elijah was an ordinary human being who did the most extraordinary things. Want to know how? He did what pleased God and he prayed. 'The effective, fervent prayer of a righteous man avails much' (Jas 5:16).

Prayer releases faith to move mountains, be they physical, spiritual or psychological. If we want to be men and women of real faith today then we must devote ourselves to prayer. The connection between our prayerlessness and the relative absence of the miraculous is no accident.

Prayerwalking is a reality. We already have reports of numerous church groups doing it in different parts of this country, as well as from abroad. It's about to become a way of life for multitudes of believers.

Is your appetite awakened? Then it's time we explained how prayerwalking actually works.

Prayer problem-solver   **3**

Where should I pray?

The early church did nearly everything outside. Solomon's portico was a favourite meeting place in Jerusalem. They also used homes. They possessed no other buildings and certainly would not have called them churches even if they had. The Greek word *ecclesia* (which means 'church') can only ever apply to people and never to a pile of bricks and mortar.

We know that Jesus often prayed outdoors and took regular prayerwalks into lonely places for that express purpose.

How Does Prayerwalking Work?

Prayerwalking is simplicity itself. In essence it is no more than the conscious combination of two of our most natural and basic human abilities: namely, walking and talking.

You don't have to be a preacher or an inveterate chatterbox, nor do you have to be an Olympic long-distance walker to participate. Almost anyone can do it. Adults, teenagers, children, the elderly and even many disabled people can take part. Your denominational background is no barrier. Race, sex and class don't even enter into the picture. Prayerwalking is a universal, international, cross-cultural Christian activity.

Prayerwalking consists of three simple elements. They are that you should be:

OUTSIDE — ON THE MOVE — TALKING TO GOD

Outside

Prayerwalking can be done almost anywhere: inner city, suburbs, town or country. The most effective will be in your immediate neighbourhood.

Weather conditions need not normally be a hindrance. Let commonsense prevail! A bit of wind and rain seldom did anybody harm, but there is no need for heroics, unless you feel especially called to it.

Any time of day or night is suitable for this perfectly legal exercise. Part of the beauty of prayerwalking is its sheer flexibility.

There is no need for heroics . . .

Get out of the car park

Christians who don't pray are like cars without petrol – miracles of divine technology parked powerless in the ecclesiastical garage when they could be unleashed on the open road to glory.

On the move

Don't imagine that prayerwalking is just for hikers. A short afternoon stroll can become a powerful prayer time, quite as much as a prayer marathon lasting several weeks. Most people can happily average a speed of about 2-3mph (3-4 kph) and make their prayerwalk last from twenty minutes to an hour. Even five minutes is better than nothing. It's not the distance you cover that counts, but the effectiveness of your praying.

The pace doesn't have to be continuous in any case. Frequent stops can be used to good advantage, and it may well be in a built-up area that you will want to stop – perhaps outside particular buildings in order to pray for the activities within them, eg, local government offices, schools.

Except on prayer pilgrimages, no special clothing is required. The aim of prayerwalking is not to draw attention to yourselves, but to seek God's face. In the same way, banners are only appropriate for certain types of major prayerwalk.

No special clothing is required . . .

Talking to God

Prayerwalking can be undertaken solo, but it is most profitable in the company of others. We recommend a typically conversational style of praying in groups of twos and threes. There is no real need to raise your voice and

There is no need to shout

passers-by may just assume that you are having a conversation with friends – even if they do catch some strange snippets as they pass you!

The simplest strategy is to go for a walk with one or two others, briefly discuss what you want to pray about and then begin to converse with the Lord. As with any conversation, it's quite legitimate to interchange between speakers and to interject your agreement while someone is praying. When the burden has been expressed, you can talk about the next thing on your hearts and repeat the process.

Because prayer is the true expression of our souls, a sense of fellowship quickly develops on a prayerwalk, even with folk who until now have been perfect strangers. Once that happens, prayer flows very freely indeed and any sense of oddness about praying on the move is soon dispelled by the sheer delight of sharing such communion with the Lord and his people.

Dad, it's me!

Spiritual life begins with prayer. That pent-up yearning of the soul which in one way or another cries, 'Jesus, I believe. Lord, save me!' is like the first breath of a new-born baby. It's the sign of spiritual life. Someone is actually there listening to us. We are communicating with God himself. No wonder Christians like praying!

Christianity is all to do with our relationship with the Lord. Eternal life is to 'know you, the only true God, and Jesus Christ whom you have sent' (Jn 17:3). A key promise of the New Covenant is that 'all shall know me, from the least of them to the greatest of them' (Heb 8:11). Sound doctrine, ardent service and charismatic gifts mean nothing apart from this. Jesus said, 'Many will say to me on that day, "Lord, Lord, have we not prophesied in your name, cast out demons in your name, and done many wonders in your name?" And then I will declare to them, "I never knew you; depart from me, you who practise lawlessness!"' (Mt 7:22-23).

If communication is essential to relationships, and prayer is how we communicate with God, then we should ensure that our Father hears from us pretty often!

Quite often, the things you observe as you walk will themselves stimulate prayer. It's quite amazing how God releases the imagination on prayerwalks and something simple like a tree or an advertising hoarding will start off a fresh train of intercession. Sometimes the Lord will lay on your heart particular people whom you pass in the street, or specific houses. You may not know until you reach heaven just what part your prayers played in their lives. The Spirit of God just wanted you to pray for them. Exciting, isn't it?

You can have periods of silent prayer, times when you agree to walk alone, occasions when you speak in tongues (if you do). It is quite proper to

worship the Lord and even sing, if that comes naturally. Some Christians get very excited in prayer and do want to shout. That's fine, provided you are sensitive towards your shyer brethren. The open road is the best place for prayer thundercrackers!

If you are part of a group then it is quite a good idea to pray with different people within the group from time to time. This often happens quite naturally in any case, particularly if you have periodic stops in order to pray all together.

Talking to God involves all forms of prayer: worship, thanksgiving, praise, intercession, supplication, declaration, confession, petition. It may also be an act of spiritual warfare. Jesus spoke of the necessary binding of the strong man before his goods could be spoiled (Mk 3:27). In one sense that was accomplished through the Incarnation; in another, it has to be implemented by the church as Christ incarnate in every generation and situation. Prayer warfare constitutes an important part of this process.

Such prophetic actions may include the spiritual cleaning out of areas known to be strongly influenced by Satan. For example, local Christians have gathered to pray from time to time at Beachy Head in Sussex because of the large number of suicides which occur from that cliff-top. Known curses may be broken by such praying. Blessing may be released in its place. Hardened areas can be opened up to the gospel. Indeed, prayerwalking of this kind would seem to be a vital precursor to the planting of new churches. We know of more than one large and effective church which was commenced by such means.

You will find yourself stirred as you contemplate rows of houses, estates and crowds of people. Like Jesus, you will feel compassion for them, for they

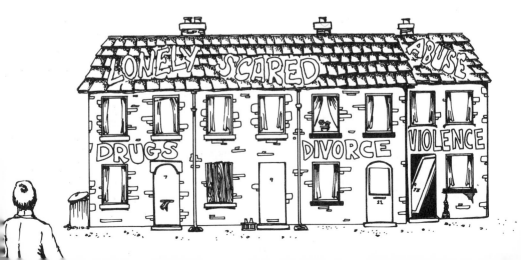

are like sheep without a shepherd. God will stir you to pray for all the broken homes and abused children, for the lonely and forsaken, for disillusioned teenagers on drugs, for the sick and the sad, for the bereaved, for the frightened and the worried. There is a world full of need out there. It needs our prayers for its deliverance.

In the last part of this manual you will find a number of self-explanatory Prayer Plans designed to enhance the effectiveness of street praying. We encourage you to take this manual with you and to use them, but don't forget, the essential cycle remains simplicity itself:

WALK AND TALK – WALK AND PRAY – WALK AND MEDITATE

— 7 —
Types of Prayerwalk

For practical purposes these fall into four categories.

1. During the normal business of life

Since prayerwalking is a way of redeeming time, we can take certain of our regular daily activities and fill them with divine significance. Here are a few ideas. You may be able to think of others.

★ Walk to or from school with your child and get a few other Christian mums to join you. Instead of talking about everyday things, pray together.

★ When you walk the dog, join with another dog walker to spend the time praying.

★ When you are in the checkout queue at the supermarket (or any other waiting situation for that matter, eg bus stops, airport terminals, railway stations) spend the time praying instead of growing frustrated. If you walk home from the shops, try to team up with a friend and pray on the journey home.

. . . when you walk the dog

★ Prayerwalk the corridors of your workplace, especially if it is an institution like a hospital, prison or school. We know one Christian headteacher of a large comprehensive school who does this whenever she senses unrest. She continues until she has brought the school under spiritual authority again and peace returns.

★ Agree once a week to walk to work with other Christians (or part of the way if it is too far) and spend the time praying.

★ One church we know of encourages members to spend half-an-hour prayerwalking their neighbourhood and praying for every house once a week from 6.45–7.15am.

★ When you are on holiday, pray with your companion as you walk around the sights.

★ Take an evening stroll with your spouse or a friend instead of watching the TV. Pray for your locality.

2. Planned small group activity

★ Prayerwalking is an ideal activity for a house group. It can be a regular part of the evening's activity, say the first half-hour, or an occasional exercise. In fact, almost any meeting can be adapted to include prayerwalking like this.

★ Why not take the regular church prayer meeting out onto the streets? You may feel it is right to do this every week, or some weeks, or part indoors and part outdoors.

★ If you have enough helpers you can on occasions take the whole Sunday School out for a prayerwalk. This can work especially well using one of the more detailed Prayer Plans provided at the end of this manual.

★ You could start an additional weekly or monthly prayerwalk. One way is for all the men and women who work in town to use their lunch break once a week in order to prayerwalk together. Fasting is optional!

★ The young people's group can go out prayerwalking. One good way is to send them off in mixed groups of half a dozen at one-minute intervals over a prescribed route. This can be made more interesting and challenging for them by giving each member a sealed envelope containing a prayer theme and a time when it is to be opened and read out.

★ If you are a student, you can organise regular campus prayerwalks with other Christians, or do it as a CU.

How about prayerwalking your school?

PRAYERWALK PROFILE ...

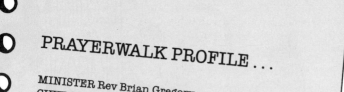

MINISTER Rev Brian Gregory
CHURCH St Nathaniel's, Platt Bridge, Wigan
AREA Anglican parish of 90 streets
TIMESPAN Past four years.
INITIATION Prayer for the Nation at Liverpool Philharmonic Hall
METHOD

Stage One

1. Divided parish streets alphabetically into prayer calendar of two per week.
2. Each week pray for 2 streets in Sunday service.
3. Each Monday deliver folded A5 leaflet to all houses in those streets. Depicts picture of Jesus on cross and the following message:

   You don't need reminding who this is, but it is in his name that we are praying for you this week. Please feel free to display this picture in a prominent place in your home to remind you of our prayers.

4. Each Wednesday 8.00 am the team for those streets meets for prayer, followed by a prayerwalk through the streets. Style is flexible, Spirit-led, sometimes includes speaking to passers-by.
5. Each week those streets are mentioned in the parish magazine for the congregation to pray over.

Stage Two

A second leaflet is delivered inviting prayer requests from local inhabitants. These are prayed for in the services and prayer meetings by members of the church. Offers to pray for people in their homes are also made.

RESULTS

Prayerwalking has become as much a characteristic of community life as the beat policeman, and has been featured in the local press.

The crime rate has dropped, the spiritual atmosphere improved and slum housing has been replaced. One policeman reports, 'Since you people have been praying for this place things have got better.'

Relationships have improved between ministers and local churches.

More people are joining the church.

PROFILE

3. Church-wide local walks

★Leaders can organise a whole church prayer invasion/saturation of an area. The aim is to mobilise every member on, say, one evening or a Sunday afternoon, perhaps finishing with a fellowship tea.

★ For even more effectiveness this can be done as a united church exercise where believers from different evangelical traditions share toge′ in prayer – a truly enriching experience! This can take the form of a 'pr′

crawl' from one church to another, spending a period of prayer at each church and then praying for its neighbourhood as you move to the next.

★ Such united exercises can be done city-wide, perhaps passing on a baton or a torch to the Christians in the next parish or administrative boundary.

. . . a prayer-crawl from one church to another . . .

★ You can easily combine such a prayerwalk with one of the Make Way Marches. Another alternative is for several churches to prayerwalk to a central rallying point, either for a Make Way March or for a Celebration, which can be held indoors or outdoors. Alternatively, the dispersal would become a multitude of prayerwalks, intelligently organised.

★ Church-wide prayerwalks can include circling a town or parish, following historic and governmental boundaries, tackling new church-planting areas, passing through large estates, praying through centres of moral evil, gathering on 'high places', especially those with occult, immoral or violent connections. In short, God wants us to go throughout the land he has set before us until his glory breaks out all over it.

The next section contains a checklist for the organising of these larger group activities.

> ### Father make us one
>
> Nothing brings Christians together more than when they truly pray. Conferences, debates and various activities are no substitute for prayer. We long for the day when the church can pray like the early church: 'They raised their voice to God with one accord and said...' (Acts 4:24).
>
> Any church characterised by a commitment to regular sustained prayer by the majority of its members will be united, purposeful and fruitful.

4. Prayer pilgrimages

★ If you feel called to pray for your nation or for your local area, you might like to take part in a pilgrimage of prayer similar to those which we and others have undertaken. Such an event may last from a few days to a few weeks. Its great merit is the sheer breadth of praying which it generates, and often national and international issues become clear in a way that is missed on the shorter walks.

★ You may feel led to prayerwalk a nation other than your own. We can foresee the formation of truly international prayerwalking teams as the precursors to continental revivals.

Prayer pilgrimages take a lot of organising and are clearly not for everyone. We have included some guidelines in this manual to assist those who might want to contemplate such a walk.

— **8** —

Organising a Group Prayerwalk

Organising a group prayerwalk requires no more than average administrative ability. Obviously, the more people involved, the greater the planning required and if your prayerwalk is an inter-church affair you will need to co-ordinate your efforts.

A simple group of two or three people who agree to do some praying, say, on the way to work, need do no more than agree a meeting place and time. Even so, some of the information given below may well be of help to make the walk more effective.

Assuming you are organising something like a house group, young people's group or church prayerwalk, the following checklist should be covered.

Organising a group prayerwalk

1. Advertising and promotion

Ensure that folk know well in advance when you intend doing the walk. It's no use blaming people for being unspiritual if you leave this until the last minute! Make sure you get it in the notices.

People need encouraging when it comes to new ventures, so the idea needs a good plug from the minister or other church leader. Ensure that everyone obtains their own copy of this book, if only for the Prayer Plans; it will help envision the group.

If you intend giving out any tracts or advertising material to interested passers-by, ensure that these are ordered well in advance, and that they are of a production quality worthy of our Lord Jesus Christ. Remember that you are required by law to include the name and address of the body responsible for distributing the material.

2. Time

This will depend on many factors, but do make sure that you choose a time people can actually manage. A bit of consultation with interested parties will help. Resist the temptation to demonstrate your spirituality by arranging times like four o'clock in the morning!

Announce not only the date and starting time, but also the finishing time. An hour's prayerwalk is probably about right for starters.

3. Route

This needs to be chosen prayerfully and may be different for every prayerwalk you undertake. Nowhere is necessarily out-of-bounds, but use wisdom when planning to go through known trouble spots.

It's amazing how many people do not know what's outside their own front door, so duplicate maps of the area and your proposed route. Insist that folk keep to it, particularly at night.

Note significant places on the route so that people are aware of where to stop and pray.

4. Clothing

Usually prayerwalking is intended to be an inconspicuous spiritual exercise, so normal everyday clothing should be worn. However, if you are walking along main roads without pavements, particularly at night, then torches and fluorescent safety jackets are strongly advised.

Do let people know what type of terrain they will be passing over. It helps if you walk the route first. Do folk need to wear stout shoes or wellington boots?

Take note of the weather. Are umbrellas and waterproofs advised?

5. Organising the group

Prayerwalking works best in groups of no more than six. One way of organising the party is to split it into such groups and send them out at one-minute intervals, all following the same route. Done like this, you should not need police permission, although if there are a large number of you it might be polite to inform them of your activity.

Alternatively, you may set off as one big group and let pace and natural relationships determine the pattern.

It is important to exercise wisdom in the construction of the group, especially to make sure that any vulnerable members, particularly children, are competently led and protected.

Count up the numbers of people setting out, and count them again at the end. These two numbers should agree!

6. Police permission

You do not need permission from the police to walk the streets with one or two friends, praying as you go. You are doing nothing illegal unless you create a public nuisance of some kind, or cause an obstruction to the pavement or public highway.

However, if you are organising a larger prayerwalk where you will all be setting off together, then you will need to inform your local constabulary. If your route involves hazardous points such as narrow unpaved roads you will need to consult with them sympathetically on how best to handle this. Police in democratic countries are generally helpful if you adopt a co-operative rather than a confrontational stance when dealing with them.

7. Briefing the participants

However well folk have read this book (!) it will still help if you explain just what they are going to be doing on the prayerwalk.

In particular:

★ Explain the route and timing.

★ Encourage those taking part not to spend the whole time talking to one another about issues, but to get on with praying as soon as possible.

★ Advise your group on particular prayer needs. It helps if these are written down. We have provided some blank pages for this purpose.

★ Explain any promptings of the Spirit which folk have been receiving and any scriptural theme for the event.

★ Let the participants know which Prayer Plan you want them to implement.

★ Remind those taking part of protocol. Behaviour should be polite and sensitive. Shouting down a residential road at 9.00pm is not appropriate. It is an offence in most countries to cause hazard to traffic by obstructing roads. The same goes for pavements. Praying against undesirable premises also needs to be handled with discretion. Our task is not to be a nuisance – at

Praying against undesirable premises also needs discretion

least, not in the visible realm! One responsible person should be appointed to whom the police should be directed in the event of them enquiring as to what you are doing.

★ Encourage people to write down anything which they feel is of special significance on the prayerwalk, be that words from the Lord, issues for follow-up, prayer issues, or opportunities spotted.

★ Launch the prayerwalk with a brief time of prayer, committing the activity to the Lord.

8. Après-pray

A prayerwalk is a venture, and as with any such venture it's a good idea to get together afterwards to compare notes and swap stories over refreshments. So organise a meeting point afterwards and lay on drinks and nibbles. Give opportunity for people to share their experiences.

Give thanks—with a grateful heart

One of the basic sins of secular society is its refusal to give thanks to God. By contrast, we believers are called to live for the praise of his glory. But if we don't ask and receive, how shall we give thanks? Philippians 4:6 says, 'Be anxious for nothing, but in everything by prayer and supplication, with thanksgiving, let your requests be made known to God.'

God delights to answer prayer so that we might have reason to celebrate with thanksgiving his goodness towards us.

If you are speaking in tongues ask God to give you (or someone else) the interpretation.

— 9 —
Planning a Prayer Pilgrimage

Walkers enjoy walking like ducks enjoy water. So the idea of a few days or weeks walking many miles across variegated countryside has a natural appeal to some, in the same way that others like to spend their time canoeing or sailing. Combining your hobby with prayer seems a marvellous idea, but a prayer pilgrimage is much more than this.

Walkers enjoy walking

★ It is a deliberate withdrawal from normal life in order to undertake a spiritual exercise of tremendous personal value.

★ It is a concentrated period of day-long intercession while on the move, praying for local, national and international issues.

★ It is a team experience in spiritual warfare, coming to grips with the principalities and powers in heavenly places and pressing through to victory.

★ It is a disciplined testing of a person's total resources, physical, mental and spiritual, over a sustained period.

★ It is a prophetic statement of our determination to pray down revival blessing upon the nation.

★ It is a vision-expanding experience not to be missed – provided you are reasonably fit!

A prayer pilgrimage needs planning if it is to be successful. The more people taking part, the greater the organisation required.

Assuming a core team of six to ten people walking for a week or longer, we provide below some guidelines as to what is involved.

1. Selection of team

A team needs to be chosen on the basis of some level of relationship. Ensure you meet together several times before the pilgrimage in order to get to know one another. A good team has a mixture of temperaments, is fairly mature and contains at least one 'pastoral' figure. Choose people who are characterised by naturalness, honesty, humour and reality.

A good team has a mixture of temperaments

2. Training

If there is any health doubt, a doctor's advice should be sought as to the suitability of a person participating.

Diet, if necessary, to reduce excess baggage. The easiest way to lose weight in anticipation of a pilgrimage is as follows: eat only whole cereal for breakfast, miss out your midday meal and supper, eat no biscuits, sugar, cake, ice-cream, chocolate, butter/margarine, puddings, but eat a normal evening main course with plenty of everything, especially vegetables, until you reach your desired weight. There are harder ways!

Although feet and legs have to be fit, overall fitness is important, especially in the lower back and abdomen. Flexibility is as important as strength, and exercise regimens should reflect this.

A daily run (eg two miles) or distance swim (one mile) will tone you up and strengthen your cardio-vascular system. Walk everywhere you can and fit in at least one long walk a week, a twenty-miler if possible. Rowing, light weight training, trunk curls, stretches, etc will take care of the rest.

Feet can be toughened by soaking them in alum, tannic acid or methylated spirits and salt. Toe-nails should be cut and cleaned a week before the walk commences. Any corns or similar disorders should be treated immediately.

Spiritual training involves spending plenty of time in prayer and the Word. Undertaking several local prayerwalks will help get you in the mood! Reading good devotional literature and books on revival is recommended.

You also need to ensure that you are well abreast of what is going on in the world. After all, you will be praying about many of these events.

3. Administration

A prayer pilgrimage of any size and duration needs the skills of a good administrator. Planning may need to begin as much as nine months in advance. You will need an administrator as part of the on-the-road team.

If you have trouble waking up to pray, put the alarm clock at a distance from your bed so you have to get up to turn it off.

4. Advance planning

The administrator will need to take care of the following:

Overnight accommodation for the team

This may be in hotels and guest houses, or on campsites, in mobile homes, motor caravanettes, or with local Christians. With regard to the latter, precisely what is needed should be made clear before an offer of hospitality is accepted, ie meals, baths, laundry, bedding, privacy, timing.

The route

This needs to be carefully planned and measured exceedingly accurately by someone driving the whole length of it. No estimating should be allowed because an unexpected extra mile or two at the end of a day can be

The route needs to be measured by someone driving the whole length of it

devastating. Average distance per day should not exceed twenty miles (thirty kilometres). Fifteen to seventeen (twenty-two to twenty-five kilometres) is better. Routes need to be planned with the co-operation of local police forces. Where possible, avoid fast, noisy main roads and busy, narrow, twisting roads.

Publicity and identification

This ranges from the advertising carried by the support vehicles to setting up local media contacts. It includes fund-raising for the event and generally making it known among the churches.

Try to engage the co-operation of local churches on the route. They can best provide 'native' guides as to the spiritual situation of their locality. Anticipated rallies and local Christians joining your walk also need organising.

Support vehicles

You will need at least three vehicles on the road, and radio contact between them and the walkers. There must be sufficient vehicles to pick up all the walkers in one go and one vehicle must provide sufficient space for an injured or exhausted walker to lie down.

5. Recommended clothing

Footwear

The best for the job are lightweight walking boots such as Hi-Tech Matterhorn or Trail with additional full Sorbothene inserts. Ordinary trainers lack sufficient ankle support. Normal mountain-walking boots are too heavy and inflexible. Forget the wellies and plimsolls!

Two pairs of socks are advisable: normal thin cotton or wool/nylon mix under heavy boucle-knit eg Lakeland Superloop.

Boots should be fitted wearing both pairs of socks. Correct fit is when you can kick the toe down on the floor and insert a finger between the boot and your ankle.

Trousers

Track-suit bottoms are very comfortable provided they are loose-fitting and made of a material with a high cotton (70%+) content.

Jeans are OK only if loose-fitting and well worn in. They are pretty awful in the wet, however. Shorts are fine, but must fit without chafing, eg Adidas sports shorts.

Walking breeches or trousers are excellent, but can get hot.

Undergarments: cotton, comfortable, any colour you like!

Upper body

The secret of comfort is several thin layers, removed as required. Walking is very hot and sweaty work!

Vest optional, but aertex, string or Damart.

Brushed-cotton shirt, open weave top, T-shirt or sweat-shirt.

Track-suit top (70%+ cotton) and/or thin woollen cardigan.

Windproof jacket, preferably fluorescent.

SAVILE ROW BESPOKE TAILORY

Wet weather gear

Gor-tex cagoules and overtrousers are ideal, but very expensive. Next down are full-proofed, eg Berghaus Monsoon. Campari-type showerproofs are unsuitable.

Headgear

Sunglasses with UV block are useful. Those with receding hair may want to wear a cotton hat. Earplugs can be helpful if it is windy.

A daysac for light personal needs is sufficient luggage on the march.

6. Food

The team should have control of its own catering. The cook (or the hosts, if you are using local hospitality) needs to work on the following: the dietary requirements for the walk should be high protein, high carbohydrate, moderate fat, high fibre. Food should be freshly cooked wherever possible. All items should be wholemeal, unprocessed and additive free. Calorie intake should be in the order of 3000-4000 per person per day.

Breakfast
This should be substantial and should ideally include wholemeal cereal or muesli. Bacon, sausages and eggs are digested slowly and can make some people feel sick for hours. Beans are best, and tomatoes, good beefburgers, fish fingers, and spaghetti are fine.

This can be followed by wholemeal toast and marmalade and tea or coffee.

Lunch
This should be light: sandwiches, wholemeal chewy bars, fruit, tea or coffee.

Chewy bars are better than sweets when walking as they give a steadier release of energy. Mars bars or glucose tablets are useful if you are feeling really drained.

Evening meal
This should be a substantial three/four course meal. Soup, with plenty of wholemeal bread, should be followed by a main course which is high in protein and has plenty of fresh vegetables. A who-cares-about-the-calories pudding can be followed by cheese and biscuits and tea or coffee.

Extra salt should be taken with the evening meal.

Supper
This could be fruit cake and biscuits, with your favourite nightcap.

Dehydration can be a problem

Dehydration can be a problem and additional fluids will be needed. The amount will vary from a minimum of one litre per person during the walk if it is cold and wet, to three or four litres per person if it is hot, dry and sunny. Best drinks are water with just a dash of pure lemon juice, or tea/coffee. Sweet canned drinks make you feel thirsty. Drink is best carried in empty transparent lemonade bottles as they weigh almost zero and impart no bad taste.

Alcohol is best avoided until the end of the day's walk. In moderation it can aid muscle relaxation, but you may feel you want to abstain for the duration of the walk for spiritual reasons.

7. Support team

Once the walk has started, a home-base support team should continue to function as a channel for communication and prayer. Some administrative matters can be handled by such a team, but the majority should be passed over to the walkers and the on-the-road administrator. This should include a set budget figure for eventualities.

It's helpful to have a simple commissioning service, inviting local leaders to participate.

On the road you will need one person responsible for organising the walking party. This should be someone with some experience of leading walkers. He/she will determine the daily timetable, speed, rest periods and the general morale of the walkers.

You will also need your administrator to handle the movements of the support vehicles, keeping in constant radio contact, ensuring food and drink supplies are adequate, taking care of emergencies, liaising with the media, checking overnight accommodation and generally being at the disposal of the walkers.

8. Communication

The state of your communication system will make or mar a prayer pilgrimage. People need to know what is going on.

Beforehand

Let people know what you are planning. Walkers need to receive minutes of planning meetings so that they can comment. Churches need to know how the arrangements are going and to be made aware of the spiritual vision behind the walk.

'I vill say zis only once . . .'

On the walk

Daily briefings should keep everyone up-to-date with progress. The front and rear walkers should both be equipped with a two-way radio. Prayer groups back at churches should receive regular bulletins.

Afterwards

A debriefing meeting should be held to ascertain the impact of the pilgrimage.

You will need to establish a policy regarding the media. Local Christians may well contact their radio, TV and newspapers, so it is as well to be prepared. A spokesperson should be appointed and a clearly written press release prepared. This should simply state the facts about the walk in no more than one side of A4 paper – the media do their own creative writing! When being interviewed, keep it light and friendly. The local media are seldom confrontational.

Back-up vehicles should carry clearly written signs advertising the walk.

Fasting from the telephone

9. Daily schedules

A prayer pilgrimage is a form of fasting, ie it is setting yourself apart from normal routines for a spiritual purpose. The team should agree on what they want to fast from, eg the telephone, work, sex, alcohol. It is unwise to do without food for any length of time while on a strenuous walk, but you may decide to miss the occasional meal.

The daily schedule should begin bright and early with a team briefing and a time of worship and prayer. Someone may profitably share a brief devotional word. The briefing should include details about the route, distance, points of interest, people you anticipate meeting, and a review of the condition of the team.

Prayer patterns will tend to evolve naturally, people praying with those who walk at the same pace as themselves. However, some moving around should be encouraged. Sometimes the police will insist that walkers are spaced out in pairs on busy roads. There should be plenty of opportunity for boisterous praise and fervent worship together as you walk and you might even find a competent musician can create a Pied Piper effect and draw others in.

If you intend meeting local Christians, give them an estimated time of arrival, but don't be pressured by that. If you are delayed they should come to meet you. Make sure you give local believers a warm welcome and explain the process of prayerwalking to them, including safety aspects on the road, especially if children have joined you.

If there are no pavements, you should always walk facing the oncoming traffic, except on blind bends where you have to use discretion. Back-up vehicles should leapfrog every two miles and carry clearly visible warnings for motorists approaching from both directions. If light or conditions are bad then walkers should wear fluorescent safety jackets.

10. Health care

Medication

Faith in God, divine protection and healing as required, together with the faith-filled use of God's providential gifts, for example, suitable medication – this is the spiritually comprehensive approach!

The pattern is likely to be one of a few aches and pains, tiredness and digestion problems over the first two or three days followed by feeling fitter and fitter as the days pass, provided there are no injuries or really bad blisters. Emotionally, the first few days of a third week may be difficult (missing loved ones, the road goes on for ever, underlying tiredness, etc.), but the end will cheer you all! Honesty about health problems is better than silent heroics.

The following comprises a typical basic personal medical kit:

Vaseline	Aspirin
Talcum powder	Cold relief tablets
Needle	Eye-drops
Plasters (non-waterproof)	Crepe bandage
Embrocation	Tissues
Diarrhoea tablets	Toe-nail clippers
Indigestion tablets	Tweezers
Sting relief spray	Lip salve
Antiseptic cream	Earplugs
Vitamin C tablets	Blister kit

Your group should include at least one qualified first-aider or person with medical experience. Blessed are you if you also have a qualified physiotherapist! The rule of the road is safety first. You should create an environment where nobody feels they have got to prove a point.

Folk become poorly when morale drops. This may be due to exhaustion, dehydration, lack of sleep, spiritual depression or foot troubles. The latter tends to be a downward spiral and prevention is better than cure. Rubbing the feet with Vaseline, changing socks round periodically and treating blisters early will help. Remember, all blisters are actually heat burns, so keep the feet as cool as possible by having regular short stops. The impact of hard roads actually generates heat. If blisters do become bad then you need to lay the victim off walking for a couple of days. He will not recover otherwise.

Spiritual health

Prayerwalking is spiritually very safe indeed. After all, we believers are at our strongest when we pray. It's a lie to suggest that you are in real danger now that you have engaged the Enemy. Our real danger is when we don't engage, because he is going to anyway! Having said that, stresses can arise between walkers, particularly if plans go amiss. Keep short accounts and encourage a speedy resolution of the problem, certainly before sundown.

Unwinding

Recovery rates for daily tiredness vary according to individual fitness, but aim to stop walking by, say, 5.00 pm to allow the maximum time. Folk also need opportunity to unwind psychologically. So, especially in the early days, don't pack in too many evening meetings and in any event don't promise to stay right through local rallies. You have a long walk tomorrow!

Prayer problem-solver   4

What do I need to believe?

Doctrine is a vital part of being a Christian, because doctrine is to do with the truth. Jesus said, 'You shall know the truth, and the truth shall make you free' (Jn 8:32). Many Christians struggle in prayer precisely because they don't really know what they believe. Let's clarify a few relevant doctrinal matters.

(a) THE TRINITY.
To whom do we pray: the Father, the Son or the Holy Spirit? Tidy theology would say that we pray to the Father, through the Son and by the Holy Spirit. That is essentially correct. The great privilege of being a Christian is to be able to call God 'our Father'. Jesus is the mediator through whom we are able to draw near to God. Prayer is a supernatural act, so we are told in Scripture to pray at all times in the Spirit.

Having said all that, you can just as easily pray to Jesus. You can even call on the Holy Spirit for help. As you grow in prayer experience you will find that you speak to all three Persons of the Trinity without any real problems. It just seems natural to address one or the other according to how we are praying at the time. (You will see evidence of this in the set prayers near the end of this book.)

(b) JUSTIFICATION BY FAITH.
Every true Christian at times feels unworthy to approach God because of a sense of failure and unholiness. It's tempting at those moments not to pray, but to go away until we feel better. God reminds us that his Son died in order that we would always find acceptance with him.

The doctrine of justification by faith, though no excuse for unholy living, provides a secure ground of acceptance for us, however we feel. 'Therefore, having been justified by faith, we have peace with God through our Lord Jesus Christ, through whom also we have access' (Rom 5:1). 'Therefore, brethren, having boldness to enter the Holy Place by the blood of Jesus ... let us draw near with a true heart in full assurance of faith' (Heb 10:19, 22).

(c) THE HOLY SPIRIT.

Prayer should always be in the Spirit. The reason is obvious: talking out loud to someone invisible isn't going to achieve very much. Prayer is a spiritual activity and needs spiritual power. Romans 8:26 says, 'Likewise the Spirit also helps in our weaknesses. For we do not know what we should pray for as we ought, but the Spirit himself makes intercession for us with groanings which cannot be uttered.'

In other words, power-assisted praying! Our prayers need never just hit the ceiling. A little cry from us, like a touch on the steering, and the power of the Holy Spirit is released to wing our prayers powerfully to the throne of God.

Praying in the Spirit may include speaking in tongues, but it is not one and the same as speaking in tongues. The latter is called 'praying with the spirit' (1 Cor 14:15), and refers to the believer's own spirit. That is an option—praying 'in the [God's] Spirit' is an essential.

(d) AUTHORITY.

'What right do you have to pray? How dare you claim that you can get God to do things when you ask? Surely you are being arrogant!'

Not at all! Every Christian is given the authority of priesthood in the name of Jesus. The Book of Hebrews tells us that Jesus is a High Priest after the order of Melchisedek. It's one of the most important truths in the New Testament. Not least, it means that he is the mediator of a New Covenant based on salvation by grace and not by works of the law.

It also means that all his people are priests and, therefore, have authority to approach the Father. We do not have to feel afraid to ask. Jesus himself gave us the right to use his name in prayer (Jn 14:13). We have been given the use of his personalised key.

(e) THE WILL OF GOD.

Many Christians feel confused about this. 'How can I pray? I don't know what God wants. Suppose I ask for the wrong things? I must do that an awful lot because most of my prayers don't seem to be answered.'

Later on in this book we suggest that you use the Lord's Prayer as a basis for your praying. Jesus gave it to us so that we would know how God wants us to pray. So no Christian ever need be in complete confusion about the will of God.

We also want to recommend that you pray with an open Bible. The more you do so, the more you will discover what the will of God is. He never shouts. The closer we draw to him and his word, the more we shall become sensitive to what he wants. Getting it right comes with practice.

Praying is not a random exercise. When you engage in a prayerwalk it's important to have some idea of what you are going to pray about. With this in mind we have provided here several frameworks designed to enhance your praying and to make it more effective. Some will appeal to you more naturally than others because of the church tradition you come from.

However, we would encourage you to give them all a try some time. Remember, personal preferences of style do not necessarily make one form of praying more spiritual than another!

In any event, these plans are designed to allow plenty of creative space, while giving a sense of direction and purpose. Experience teaches us that even the most freewheeling pray-er appreciates a little encouragement and direction along the way.

Do remember that one of the great merits of prayerwalking is that you encounter real streets, real houses and real people. These are the raw materials for your praying, so be specific – 'earth' your heavenly prayers!

Plan one: Free-flight

This is a plan to assist those used to 'free-flight', or extempore praying. To some extent it will form a part of all the prayer plans.

The great strength of such praying is that it allows a ready response to the immediate situation and puts a strong emphasis on 'being led by the Spirit' in prayer. It is not without its weaknesses, however. Sustained extempore prayer requires a fair degree of mental and verbal flexibility, as well as concentration and stamina, if we are not to dry up after a few minutes. Many Christians confess concerning their personal devotional times, 'I can't think of anything more to say after three or four minutes.' Such folk may well quail at the idea of half-an-hour of sustained praying out loud, even if shared with others.

Free-flight praying does not always hit the target either. If we are not careful, 'led by the Spirit' degenerates into haphazard praying for anything that comes into our heads. At the end, we might just wonder what we have achieved.

With this in mind, we want to suggest some simple ideas to focus our praying.

The easiest pattern is for a small group of between two and six people to walk, and to talk for a few minutes about what is on their hearts, then to turn these burdens into prayer. It's important, particularly with inexperienced intercessors, not to allow talking about the issue to go on too long. All that is required is that the heart burden is communicated. A time of praying together might then be followed by a short period when you walk in personal communion with the Lord. Some may wish to pray quietly, in their usual language or their prayer language, during such periods.

Either something you see, or some fresh burden, may provoke you to begin praying again, or you may want briefly to talk about the matter with your companions before praying. Experienced pray-ers will generally feel very comfortable with this style. It can be enhanced by several useful ideas:

1. Stop at various times and gather for prayer as a little group. You might favour a local landmark, or civic institutions such as town halls, schools and police stations as appropriate places. Or, of course, outside church buildings. Other places include pubs, clubs, discos, premises used by cults, sports stadiums, prisons, military establishments, key industrial sites and hospitals.

2. God's word is the best stimulus to prayer and we suggest you carry a Bible with you. If you don't want to get run over, it's best to read Scripture while stationary! Appropriate scriptures addressed to your little prayer group provide fresh fuel for 'free-flight' praying.

> **Keep a notebook to record special requests and their answers.**

Don't get bogged down looking for obscure passages with prophetic revelation for the occasion. These may be forthcoming, but what you are really after are scriptures which encourage and inspire. Dipping into the Psalms is almost always successful. Here are a few classic references in addition to the Psalms:

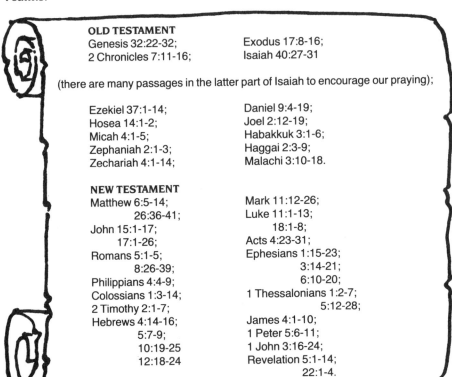

OLD TESTAMENT

Genesis 32:22-32;   Exodus 17:8-16;
2 Chronicles 7:11-16;   Isaiah 40:27-31

(there are many passages in the latter part of Isaiah to encourage our praying);

Ezekiel 37:1-14;   Daniel 9:4-19;
Hosea 14:1-2;   Joel 2:12-19;
Micah 4:1-5;   Habakkuk 3:1-6;
Zephaniah 2:1-3;   Haggai 2:3-9;
Zechariah 4:1-14;   Malachi 3:10-18.

NEW TESTAMENT

Matthew 6:5-14;   Mark 11:12-26;
    26:36-41;   Luke 11:1-13;
John 15:1-17;   18:1-8;
    17:1-26;   Acts 4:23-31;
Romans 5:1-5;   Ephesians 1:15-23;
    8:26-39;   3:14-21;
Philippians 4:4-9;   6:10-20;
Colossians 1:3-14;   1 Thessalonians 1:2-7;
2 Timothy 2:1-7;   5:12-28;
Hebrews 4:14-16;   James 4:1-10;
    5:7-9;   1 Peter 5:6-11;
    10:19-25   1 John 3:16-24;
    12:18-24   Revelation 5:1-14;
    22:1-4.

3. It will assist such praying if you note down specific matters to pray about beforehand, and if you keep a record of the major requests actually made during your prayerwalk. After all, if you don't remember what you asked, you can hardly thank God when he answers! There are blank pages at the back of this book which can be used for this purpose. Get in the habit of noting down the date you asked and the date God answered. You'll be amazed at just how many prayers are specifically answered over a period of time.

Those used to receiving words of prophecy from the Lord might also care to record such words for future reference.

4. If you are praying through a residential area, rather than simply praying for every house in a street, you might feel you should pray discreetly for specific homes as you pass them. Do be sensible about this or you may have the local Neighbourhood Watch phoning the police! However, if you are truly open to the Holy Spirit this need not be a random exercise. You may well have the joy of seeing your prayers answered very specifically indeed! Don't be afraid to note down specific house numbers that you prayed for.

If you are praying for your own road or block of flats, think specifically about neighbours known to you. Do you need to forgive any of them – or to apologise, for that matter?

An extension to this is to let the Holy Spirit guide you in prayer as to which homes are to be earmarked in faith for future house groups. You may feel led to pray for the planting of a new church or some aspect of Christian outreach in a particular area. Be specific about which building to use or which homes to concentrate upon. Is God saying you should evangelise a particular club or pub?

5. Consider the possibility of following a prayer theme. For example, praying for the family life of your town, or attacking perceived spiritual strongholds, or praying for the centres of civic power – the town hall, schools, police station, social services and so on.

As suggested earlier, with a young people's group you might consider a 'sealed orders' approach where previously agreed prayer themes are enclosed in plain envelopes and distributed to each member of the group with a start time on them. When the appropriate time comes, the envelope is opened and the theme prayed about by the group until the next time slot arrives.

With a prayer theme it's very important to keep applying it to specific locations. 'Lord, we pray for all the families in this road,' is nothing like as effective as, 'Lord, we pray for the husband and wife in this house. We can see they are quite well off, but we ask that they might come into spiritual wealth by knowing you.' Start praying like this and you may find the Lord giving you revelation about that family's specific needs.

Plan two: The Lord's Prayer

The Lord's Prayer was given by Jesus as a pattern for our praying. Although it is perfectly all right simply to recite the Prayer, there is another wonderfully effective way of using it, which is to consider each phrase as a 'window' into a world of prayer possibilities. This is the approach we have adopted here.

All you have to do to 'enter the window' is declare the phrase and, for a few minutes, explore the prayer world within it before moving on to the next phrase in the sequence. Such an exercise might take from half-an-hour to an hour, during which time you may have walked anything from one to three miles (2.25 to 4.5 kilometres). To help you find your way, we have included a few signposts under each phrase, based on the New King James Version of Matthew 6:9-13.

OUR FATHER IN HEAVEN
Thank God for your own 'sonship by adoption' into his family.
- ★ Worship God for his Son, Jesus, our 'elder brother'.
- ★ Pray for the Christians in the locality which you are passing through.
- ★ Pray for the people around you who do not know God as their Father.
- ★ Pray for the well-being and encouragement of family life in your town and in your nation. Don't forget the fatherless.

HALLOWED BE YOUR NAME
Declare the glory of God enshrined in his name.
- ★ Pray against all blasphemies and false gods, especially centres of false religion in your locality.
- ★ Pray for holiness and unity among his people in your area.

YOUR KINGDOM COME
Thank God that Jesus is Lord of all.
- ★ Pray for the rule of God to be acknowledged by all the institutions and authorities in your town.
- ★ Remember specific apostles (missionaries), prophets, evangelists, pastors and teachers known to you.
- ★ Pray for revival to come on the streets you are walking through.

YOUR WILL BE DONE ON EARTH AS IT IS IN HEAVEN
Submit yourself afresh to the will of God.
- ★ Ask him for his will on specific issues in your area and pray that will into being.
- ★ Pray for rulers and all in authority that they would submit to heaven's government.

GIVE US THIS DAY OUR DAILY BREAD

Thank God for his provisions.

★ Express your trust in his providential and miraculous supplies.
★ Pray for those in famine situations.
★ Pray for local environmental issues.
★ Remember your brethren who are in prison for their faith, including those who are oppressed in their own homes by unbelieving relatives.
★ Pray for the supply of spiritual bread to the population of your area.
★ Pray against local manifestations of the powers of materialism.

AND FORGIVE US OUR DEBTS

Confess any known specific sin and receive God's forgiveness.

★ Confess the sins of the church and the sins of your town.
★ Ask God to show mercy towards us.
★ Pray for the Holy Spirit to convict the local population of sin, righteousness and judgement.

AS WE FORGIVE OUR DEBTORS

Forgive those neighbours who have hurt you and pray God's blessing upon them.

★ Pray for the repentance of those who will not forgive, many of whom are ill because of it.
★ Pray for the healing of your community.

AND DO NOT LEAD US INTO TEMPTATION

Pray that we will overcome opposition and not lose our faith.

★ Pray for weak Christians known to you.
★ Remember those enduring hard trials at this time.
★ Commit yourself again to walk in the paths of righteousness.
★ Pray for specific zones of temptation in your community to be cleaned up.

BUT DELIVER US FROM THE EVIL ONE

Pray for the pulling down of satanic strongholds, locally and nationally.

★ Pray against local occultism in all its manifestations.
★ Pray for peace and protection on the streets of your town.

FOR YOURS IS THE KINGDOM AND THE POWER AND THE GLORY FOR EVER. AMEN

Rejoice in the sovereignty of God and express your confidence in him.

★ Pray that every knee would bow in worship to Jesus and that his praise would fill your community.

★ Pray for his return in glory and that multitudes around you will greet that day with joy.

———————— □ ————————

Plan three: The Ten Commandments

This one is based on the Ten Commandments. It may be used on its own or as an extended part of the Lord's Prayer 'window': *Your will be done on earth as it is in heaven.*

The Ten Commandments constitute the moral code for a nation under God. Hence they are directly applicable to the conduct of the church and its members. Love, that is love for God and our neighbours, expresses itself through obedience to these commandments (Rom 13:8-10).

In a secondary sense, these commandments also offer a moral base for the legislation of any nation which wishes to honour God. Laws based on these commandments will encourage good citizenship and discourage bad.

With this in mind, we can use the Ten Commandments as a prayer plan both for the church and for our nation. We have given suggested prayer themes under each commandment first for the church and then for the nation. You may wish to use one or the other, or both. As with the previous plan we suggest you spend an agreed few minutes on each. You'll be amazed how much your prayer life opens out and how far you will have walked!

This particular plan is well-suited to a local united churches prayerwalk. Although you seek to pray into specific local situations, this pattern is particularly useful to help you focus on national and city-wide issues.

Visual association is a great help on a prayerwalk. Advertising hoardings may well provoke you to pray. Rubbish on the streets can be a pertinent allegory of the state of souls. A flower in the gutter may remind you of hope surviving in desperate situations, or, conversely, of an abused child. Let God speak to your eyes.

Leaders of groups may like to read out the commandments at suitable intervals on the walk and so initiate a new phase of prayer.

1. YOU SHALL HAVE NO OTHER GODS

Church: ★ Pray against spiritual adultery – that tendency in the church to allow the gods of materialism, humanistic thinking and multi-faith compromises to draw her away from the centrality and simplicity of pure faith in Christ.

★ Pray for a fearless confidence in the gospel among the preachers and public representatives of the church, so that the world knows precisely where we stand as 'a community of loving defiance'.

Nation: ★ Pray for teachers of religious education in schools, that they may have clarity, courage and wisdom in presenting the uniqueness of an evangelical Christian faith in a multi-religious context.

★ Pray that our nation will be saved from materialism and from neo-pagan occultism.

2. YOU SHALL NOT MAKE FOR YOURSELF AN IDOL

Church: ★ Pray that the church be delivered from that spirit of the world which glamorises and elevates personalities at the expense of God's glory.

★ Pray against false doctrine and arid theology born out of the idolatry of the intellect. The foolishness of the cross is still the power and wisdom of God to those who believe.

Nation: ★ Pray that our society may be delivered from the worship of money with all its attendant evils.

★ Pray for young people to be protected from the false value systems of media-created pop idols and cult personalities, eg football, children's TV, New Age cartoons.

3. YOU SHALL NOT MISUSE THE NAME OF THE LORD

Church: ★ Pray for a church freed from all hypocrisy and from all that shames the name of our Lord.

★ Pray against the financial exploitation of God's people by those who would commercialise the work of grace.

Nation: ★ Pray for the failure of false messiahs and religious cults which purport to be the true Christian faith but are not.

★ Pray for the fair exercise of the blasphemy laws so that the sensibilities of Christians are respected.

4. REMEMBER THE SABBATH DAY

Church: ★ Pray that the church may be noted for its care of the sick, the weak and the needy, both by its voice of protest and by its charitable works and miraculous acts.

★ Pray for the preaching of the gospel of grace which brings a Sabbath rest to the soul.

Nation: ★ Pray for the protection of workers against exploitation by their bosses, and that the nation may enjoy a day of substantial rest and recreation.

★ Pray that people may be delivered from the stress-inducing lifestyles of our age and that they may find true well-being in the Lord.

5. HONOUR YOUR FATHER AND MOTHER

Church: ★ Pray for the protection of family relationships in the church. Especially uphold the families of leaders and active Christian workers.

★ Remember the families of missionaries and of those who are imprisoned for their faith.

Nation: ★ Pray for legislation that will protect and encourage the family unit and for the unmasking of those who would subvert it.

★ Pray for the vast numbers of fatherless children and husbandless mothers resulting from our permissive society.

6. YOU SHALL NOT MURDER

Church: ★ Pray for unity and peace within the church and a freedom from cynicism, sarcasm and gossip among members.

★ Pray for love, trust and unity among all true churches and their leaders.

Nation: ★ Pray for the exercise of just penalties on first-degree murderers, and for an uncorrupted, fair legal system.

★ Pray for the ending of mass abortion and for a revision of the abortion laws to protect the rights of the unborn child.

7. YOU SHALL NOT COMMIT ADULTERY

Church: ★ Pray for the upholding of sexual purity among God's people.

★ Pray for Christian marriages to become good role models for the future of family life.

Nation: ★ Pray for the revision of laws and economic policies which encourage immoral and unnatural relationships.

★ Pray for the curbing of the pornographic trade and other forms of sexual exploitation.

8. YOU SHALL NOT STEAL

Church: ★ Pray for financial integrity in the use of church funds and for adequate financial provision for full-time Christian workers.

★ Pray for a continual release of cheerful giving to meet the needs of the poor and destitute.

Nation: ★ Pray for enlightened government policies which will curb the economic exploitation of developing nations.

★ Pray for the exposure of fraud and corruption in high places, particularly where this is done through cartels and secret societies.

9. YOU SHALL NOT GIVE FALSE TESTIMONY

Church: ★ Pray for transparent honesty to characterise all our speech and conduct. Let us be freed from dubious political manoeuvrings in church affairs.

Nation: ★ Pray for the cleaning up of the popular media and for reporting to be characterised by fairness and integrity.

★ Pray for an open government that is not 'economical with the truth'.

10. YOU SHALL NOT COVET

Church: ★ Pray that we will not be greedy for power, ministry or fame, but will humbly serve the Lord Christ.

★ Pray for a generous sharing of Christian resources among churches and the end of selfish empire-building.

Nation: ★ Pray for economic policies which restrain greed and ensure a fair distribution of wealth.
★ Pray for the downfall of the drug trade and the syndicated crime associated with it.

Your kingdom come, your will be done on earth as it is in heaven.

Plan four: Liturgical

This plan is wholly liturgical and is designed for those whose tradition is for the meaningful reciting of set prayers. It might profitably be given a try by those from other traditions, however.

Because of the obvious difficulties usually encountered when trying to walk and read at the same time, we recommend that the written prayers are recited when stationary and that the times of walking are spent either in spiritually constructive conversation or in quiet meditation – or, of course, in extempore prayer as outlined in prayer plan one. Accordingly, the word PROCEED is used to indicate that the party should move to the next 'prayer station'. Do remember that you are walking so as to be aware of your spiritual environment. Although the set prayers are by their nature broad in wording, it is essential that your praying between these should be specifically focused on the needs around you.

The group leader should encourage each member of the group to read some part of THE ORDER.

Depending on the distance covered between the stops, this prayer plan should occupy about half-an-hour in total.

THE ORDER

Almighty God, we come to you in the name of your Son,
our Saviour, Jesus Christ.
As we seek your face in prayer,
we ask that your Holy Spirit would strengthen and guide us in our intercessions.
We pray for unity in the Spirit and effectiveness in our prayers.
May we your servants accomplish your will this day,
through Jesus Christ our Lord. Amen.

The following scriptures may then be read:

'Ask, and it will be given to you; seek, and you will find; knock, and it will be opened to you. For everyone who asks receives, and he who seeks finds, and to him who knocks it will be opened' (Lk 11:9-10).

'If you abide in me, and my words abide in you, you will ask what you desire, and it shall be done for you. By this my Father is glorified, that you bear much fruit; so shall you be my disciples' (Jn 15:7-8).

'The spirit also helps in our weaknesses. For we do not know what we should pray for as we ought, but the Spirit himself makes intercession for us with groanings which cannot be uttered' (Rom 8:26).

'Therefore, brethren, having boldness to enter the Holy Place by the blood of Jesus, by a new and living way which he consecrated for us, through the veil, that is, his flesh, and having a high priest over the house of God, let us draw near with a true heart in full assurance of faith, having our hearts sprinkled from an evil conscience and our bodies washed with pure water' (Heb 10:19-22).

The Lord's Prayer may be said together.

PROCEED

Heavenly Father, as you have reminded us to pray for those in authority, we now lift up to you our constitutional head and the members of our government.
Grant that they may seek your face for heavenly wisdom in their counsels.
May they pursue the paths of righteousness, peace and integrity.
Purge out all corruption and deceit, we beseech you.
Let justice roll down like water and righteousness like a mighty stream.
May the good of the people always be pre-eminent
in the minds of those who have the rule over us.
We ask this through Jesus Christ, Lord of all. Amen.

We thank you for our local council
and ask that our civic leaders may be men and women of integrity,
who despise corruption and serve the good of the people.
Save us from petty tyrannies,
from financial malpractice and wastefulness;

from foolish projects and vested interests.
Meet the needs of your people in the provision of buildings and in
    freedom of activity.
May a good spirit be engendered in our [town]
through the benign influence of the gospel. Amen.

At this point specific local issues may be brought to God in prayer.

Lord Jesus Christ, you are the Prince of Peace.
We ask you to extend your gracious rule of peace over all the world.
Bring to nothing the counsels of the wicked;
thwart those who by violence seek to further their own ends,
whether by the machinery of war, international terrorism,
political intimidation or police brutality.
We pray for an end to the traffic in drugs, prostitution and human
    slavery.
Give supernatural aid to those engaged in the fight against such evils.
We pray for racial harmony
and for an end to the exploitation of the poor.
May all recognise that to whom much is given, much also is required,
and act accordingly for the relief of the disadvantaged.
In your name we pray. Amen.

We remember before your throne those of our brethren
who are persecuted for righteousness' sake, and we honour them.
Will you sustain them with your grace
and bless both them and their loved ones?
Comfort them in their isolation, pain and imprisonment.
May they be often reminded that they share in the sufferings of our
    Lord.
Let them know we have not forgotten their plight,
and grant us the means of aiding them.
May the oppression of the wicked soon be broken.
We remember before you now those known to us by name.

Here, silent or extempore prayer may be offered for suffering saints.

The following scripture may be read:

'Surely his salvation is near to those who fear him, that glory may dwell in our land. Mercy and truth have met together; righteousness and peace have kissed each other. Truth shall spring out of the earth, and righteousness shall look down from heaven. Yes, the Lord will give what is good; and our land will yield its increase' (Ps 85:9-12).

Our Lord and Father, we pray for our own [town].
May your peace fill our streets and our homes.
Remove far from us the cry of distress.
Curb the activities of murderers, thieves, and rapists,
of drunkards, and those who lie in wait devising plans of violence in
    their hearts.
Even as we walk these streets
may the peace of God come upon them.
We ask this in the name of our Lord Jesus Christ. Amen.

Consider your neighbourhood and pray against known local vices.

PROCEED

The Apostles' Creed may next be said:

I believe in God, the Father almighty,
creator of heaven and earth.

I believe in Jesus Christ, his only Son,
    our Lord.
He was conceived by the power of the
    Holy Spirit
and born of the Virgin Mary.
He suffered under Pontius Pilate,
was crucified, died, and was buried.
He descended to the dead.
On the third day he rose again.
He ascended into heaven,
and is seated at the right hand
    of the Father.
He will come again to judge the living
    and the dead.

I believe in the Holy Spirit,
the holy catholic Church,
the communion of saints,
the forgiveness of sins,
the resurrection of the body,
and the life everlasting. Amen.

Our heavenly Father, it is your gospel which has brought salvation to
us, and we give you heartfelt thanks for your grace and mercy.
We pray that the truth of your gospel will permeate every stratum of
  society.
To that end we lift up to you
those who proclaim the good news of our Lord Jesus Christ.
Strengthen them, grant to them boldness of utterance,
fill them with the power of your Holy Spirit,
so that the word may be effective and accompanied by such signs and
  wonders as shall testify to the truth.
We pray in the name of him who is the truth,
our Lord Jesus Christ. Amen.

At this point, pray for God's salvation to touch the people in your immediate vicinity.

We thank you for our churches, Lord.
Though they are beset by many foes, by trials within and without,
we thank you that through your Son you have promised to build your
  church and the gates of hell shall not prevail against it.
Therefore we rejoice in tribulation
and call upon you to help us overcome our adversaries,
through the blood of Jesus and the testimony to his power.

We pray for the purity of your people:
may sin always be abhorrent to us,
and hypocrisy far from our lives.
Let love be manifest in our midst,
truth on our lips and unity of heart in our shared life together.
Through Jesus Christ, Lord of all our lives. Amen.

The following scripture may now be read:

'I do not pray for these alone, but also for those who will believe in me through their word; that they all may be one, as you, Father, are in me, and I in you; that they also may be one in us, that the world may believe that you sent me. And the glory which you gave me I have given them, that they may be one just as we are one: I in them and you in me; that they may be made perfect in one, and that the world may know that you have sent me, and have loved them as you have loved me' (Jn 17:20-23).

Father, we pray for the unity of your people.
We confess to our shame
that we have been suspicious, critical and divisive in spirit.
Lord, we repent, and ask for grace
so that the prayer of your Son might be answered.
Forgive us, Lord, for our disunity.
Help us to love our brethren
especially those from traditions and backgrounds different from our
    own.
While holding without compromise to the faith once for all delivered to
    the saints,
enable us to see beyond secondary matters which need not divide.
To this end we pray for special grace to be on our leaders,
that they may be able to distinguish between the wolves and the sheep,
and gladly receive all those who belong to you,
the Great Shepherd of the sheep. Amen.

The names of local churches may now be mentioned and prayer offered for their blessing.

PROCEED

We thank you, O Lord,
that it was your good will to establish marriage
and to set children in families.
We pray now for the wellbeing of family life in our nation.
Almighty Lord, visit failure and confusion on those who seek to destroy
    the family.
We pray against the forces of sexual permissiveness and perversity

at work through the media and educational systems of our land.
May the virtues of chastity, passionate love and marital faithfulness
  between man and woman again be upheld.
Close down the degrading trade in pornography and prostitution
and restore to proper dignity and discretion all those involved in such
  trade.
For the sake of your holy name we pray. Amen.

Here, prayer may be offered concerning local newsagents, video and bookshops, etc.

Heavenly Father, bless and protect our children,
for they are your children too.
We grieve over the plight of those who are scarred by the sins of their
  parents.
Have mercy upon those from broken homes.
May they find security in you
and a welcome in the family of God.
Bring healing to their lives, O Lord.
We remember those known to us now.

Silent or extempore prayer may now be offered for such.

Help us, Lord God, to bring an end to the cruel abuse of children.
We denounce before your throne
the needless slaughter of multitudes through abortion for convenience,
and pray for repentance and courage in medical staff
and in the families and individuals concerned.
You who see in secret,
hear the cry of children who are sexually abused and beaten.
Have mercy on them,
and turn the heart of the nation to abhor such crimes.
Heal the lives of those whose childlike trust was betrayed
and who now bear the wounds in their personalities.
We pray for all those Christian agencies involved in the rescue and
  restoration of abused children.
Lord, make them open channels of your healing love.
We pray in Jesus' precious name. Amen.

Most child abuse takes place behind innocent-looking doors. Pray for the houses in your immediate vicinity.

The following scriptures may be read:

'Open your mouth for the speechless, in the cause of all who are appointed to die. Open your mouth, judge righteously, and plead the cause of the poor and needy' (Prov 31:8-9).

'Whoever receives one little child like this in my name receives me. But whoever causes one of these little ones who believe in me to sin, it would be better for him if a millstone were hung around his neck, and he were drowned in the depth of the sea' (Mt 18:5-6).

'Let the little children come to me, and do not forbid them; for of such is the kingdom of heaven' (Mt 19:14).

Let us pray for our schools, colleges and universities.
As we do so, we are mindful of the powerful influence of education in shaping young lives.
We are also aware that little place is given to honouring God in our schools and colleges.
O Lord our God, please bring your influence to bear
through Christian educationalists, teachers and students.
We pray for the appointment of wise headteachers and principals who fear you.
We pray for further changes in the curriculum,
so that divine wisdom might again have precedent over mere knowledge.
Strengthen the hands of those involved in Christian Unions.
May such meetings be gatherings for mutual encouragement
and evangelistic outreach to fellow students.
Through the power of Jesus Christ our Lord. Amen.

Here, prayer may be offered for your local educational establishments, for known teachers and pupils.

PROCEED

We acknowledge the influence of the media
both for good and for ill.
Father, we thank you that we live in an era of easy communication.
We pray that such resources might be used wisely and nobly
for the moral and spiritual advancement of mankind.
We pray for honest, open journalism,

for the unmasking of evil and the promotion of that which is good.
Encourage your people wherever they are engaged in the
    communication industry.
We pray in the name of him who is your living Word,
our Saviour Jesus Christ. Amen.

*Prayer may now be offered for your local newspaper, radio and TV station. Note the
aerials and satellite dishes, and pray for the viewers in houses around you.*

The following scriptures may be read:

'The heavens declare the glory of God; and the firmament shows his
handiwork. Day unto day utters speech, and night unto night reveals
knowledge. There is no speech or language where their voice is not
heard. Their line has gone out through all the earth, and their words
to the end of the world.
        'The law of the Lord is perfect, converting the soul; the testimony
of the Lord is sure, making wise the simple; the statutes of the Lord
are right, rejoicing the heart; the commandment of the Lord is pure,
enlightening the eyes; the fear of the Lord is clean, enduring for ever;
the judgements of the Lord are true and righteous altogether. More
to be desired are they than gold, yea, than much fine gold' (Ps 19:1-4,
7-10).

Let your word go forth into all the earth, O Lord.
We thank you for the availability of the media for spreading the gospel.
Supply the needs of all those engaged in such activities.
We think of the Bible societies,
of Christian television and radio,
of Christian writers and publishers,
of musicians, and those involved in preaching your word.
Let the word of God have free course
and be acknowledged as the instrument for saving many from their
    sins.
Open doors previously closed,
and break down barriers to the truth of your Word.
In our generation
may every soul hear the good news of Jesus Christ.
We ask this for his name's sake. Amen.

PROCEED

Our Father, as we come to the end of our short pilgrimage, we thank you for your presence with us. We have made our requests known in Jesus' name and we believe you have seen the true desires of our hearts. Grant us what we ask, not for our own sakes, but for your eternal glory, and let us see the answers to our prayers so that we may thank and praise your holy name. Through Jesus Christ our Lord. Amen.

The Grace may be said together:

May the grace of our Lord Jesus Christ,
and the love of God,
and the fellowship of the Holy Spirit
be with us all evermore. Amen.

———————— □ ————————

Plan five: Declaration of faith

This plan is designed around the Evangelical Alliance Basis of Faith and is particularly useful for a 'truth-focused' prayerwalk. As such it encourages us to ask for the whole counsel of God to enter the lives of those for whom we pray. It may be used militantly as a declaration of truth against error.

This pattern may be used by large or small groups and is a simple one to implement. At the instigation of the group leader, the group reads the first declaration out loud in unison. The walk then gets underway and 'free-flight' praying falls into the following pattern:

★ Thanksgiving and praise for the truth which we have just declared and which has set our hearts free.

★ Prayer for the church to hold fast to this particular sound doctrine and to declare it fearlessly in the face of heresy and schism. Such prayers should include a burden for the truth concerned to adorn our lives locally and to be expressed in practical love to God and our immediate neighbours.

★ Intercession for a lost world imprisoned by the deceptions of the father of lies. Pray that the truth of the declaration you have just made may penetrate the darkness and bring salvation to sinners, particularly in your locality. Keep asking yourself the question, 'How does this truth apply to the people around here?' The transference of eternal truth to present reality is vital if our prayers are to be effective. Ask God to help you see the connections, and pray accordingly. We've included a 'trigger' question under each declaration to help you get the idea.

After five minutes of walking and praying in this fashion, you should regroup and read the second declaration out loud together. The pattern is repeated until all the declarations have been prayed through. Such a prayerwalk will take about forty-five minutes to complete.

1   FIRST DECLARATION

We declare our belief in the sovereignty and grace of God the Father, God the Son and God the Holy Spirit in creation, providence, revelation, redemption and final judgement.

Do the people in this road know who God is?

2   SECOND DECLARATION

We declare our belief in the divine inspiration of the Holy Scripture and its consequent entire trustworthiness and supreme authority in all matters of faith and conduct.

How many homes have an open Bible in a readable translation?

3 THIRD DECLARATION

We declare our belief in the universal sinfulness and guilt of fallen man, making him subject to God's wrath and condemnation.

Is the Holy Spirit convicting your community of this fact?

4 FOURTH DECLARATION

We declare our belief in the substitutionary sacrifice of the incarnate Son of God as the sole and all-sufficient ground of redemption from the guilt and power of sin, and from its eternal consequences.

Has this good news reached the people you are walking past?

5 FIFTH DECLARATION

We declare our belief in the justification of the sinner solely by the grace of God through faith in Christ crucified and risen from the dead.

Are the local churches preaching this effectively?

6 SIXTH DECLARATION

We declare our belief in the illuminating, regenerating, indwelling and sanctifying work of God the Holy Spirit.

Who rules this street—the Holy Spirit or unholy spirits?

7 SEVENTH DECLARATION

We declare our belief in the priesthood of all believers, who form the universal church, the body of which Christ is the Head, and which is committed by his command to the proclamation of the gospel throughout the world.

Is this what they believe to be true of your church in the local pubs?

8 EIGHTH DECLARATION

We declare our belief in the expectation of the personal, visible return of the Lord Jesus Christ in power and glory.

Will that person across the road be ready?

We'll walk the land
(Let the flame burn brighter)

Graham Kendrick

Capo 3 (D)

With a strong rhythm

Verse

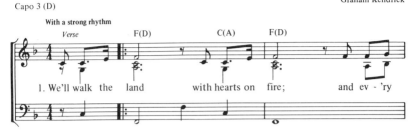

1. We'll walk the land with hearts on fire; and ev - 'ry

step will be a prayer. Hope is ris - ing, new day

dawn - ing; sound of sing - ing fills the air.

2. Two thou - sand   Let the flame burn

2. Two thousand years, and still the flame
   Is burning bright across the land.
   Hearts are waiting, longing, aching,
   For awakening once again.

3. We'll walk for truth, speak out for love;
   In Jesus' name we shall be strong,
   To lift the fallen, to save the children,
   To fill the nation with Your song.

PRAYER REQUESTS AND ANSWERS

PRAYERS

ANSWERS

PRAYERS

ANSWERS

Graham Kendrick
MAKE WAY
Series

These products will provide an essential resource for all those considering 'Make Way' style events, both on and off of the streets.

MAKE WAY FOR THE KING – A CARNIVAL OF PRAISE.
Cassette (MWC1)
The music for this album is contained in the following songbooks:
Graham Kendrick Songbook Volume One
Graham Kendrick Songbook Volume Two

MAKE WAY FOR JESUS – SHINE JESUS SHINE.
Cassette (MWC2)
Compact Disc (MWD2)
Backing Tracks (MWT2)
Make Way Organisers' Handbook (Music Edition)
Make Way Marchers' Handbook (Words Edition)

MAKE WAY FOR CHRISTMAS – THE GIFT.
Cassette (MWC3)
Compact Disc (MWD3)
Backing Tracks (MWT3)

Songbook (with Leaders' Notes)

MAKE WAY FOR THE CROSS – LET THE FLAME BURN BRIGHTER.
Cassette (MWC4)
Compact Disc (MWD4)
Backing Tracks (MWT4)

Songbook (With Leaders' Notes)

Also by Graham Kendrick

WORSHIP (Paperback)
Whether you are a leader of worship or see yourself as playing a more passive role, this book is designed to help you experience greater depth and meaning in your highest calling – to worship the living God.

For more information on Graham Kendrick's 'Make Way Music' Ministry (including the above products) send an s.a.e. to Make Way Music, Glyndley Manor, Stone Cross, Pevensey, East Sussex, BN24 5BS.

Also by John Houghton from Kingsway . . .

So You've Got Teenage Children Too . . .

Practical advice to help you be friends with your teenage child, and improve your understanding of the pressurising culture he or she belongs to.

A Touch of Love

The world seems preoccupied with sex – but this sex manual emphasises that *love*-making involves commitment – and practice! Ideal for married couples of any age.

The Oswain Tales

From *Hagbane's Doom*, past *Gublak's Greed*, through *Surin's Revenge* and on to *Tergan's Lair*, two boys and a girl join forces with King Oswain and his servants, against the forces of darkness in a world that exists parallel to our own.

Order from your local Christian Bookshop, or in case of difficulty direct from:
The Rainbow Company, PO Box 77, Hailsham, E. Sussex BN27 3ER.